VOLCANO
INSURANCE

VOLCANO INSURANCE

The proactive approach to avoid, manage and resolve disputes

THE DISPUTE AVOIDANCE & RESOLUTION PARTNERSHIP

"This book is published at a time when, more than ever before, businesses need access to the best advice in how to avoid, manage and resolve disputes that might undermine their ability to survive and thrive in the modern world."

Jane Gunn, Mediator, Author of "How To Beat Bedlam In The Boardroom And Boredom In The Bedroom", and Chair of the Board of Management of CIArb.

"As mediators we have seen frequently the negative impact that the late resolution of disputes has on a business or an individual. For that reason, CEDR has for many years worked hard to move the conversation away from a sole focus on resolution, towards also the prevention and management of conflict and disputes. This we know was something our former distinguished colleague David Richbell also felt strongly about. It is for this reason we are sure that this Guide; Volcano Insurance, initiated by him and his fellow authors, will become an important handbook to all leaders who are seeking to use the benefit of hindsight beforehand and helping them avoid and manage disputes."

Dr Karl Mackie, Founder President of the Centre for Effective Dispute Resolution (CEDR); and James South, Managing Director of CEDR

"Few people come away from a Court room or an Arbitration hearing recommending it to their friends as an incredible process for dispute resolution. Those who sensibly decide to try Mediation before taking the final step towards a court, are warned that they will be unlikely to skip and dance down the street, even if settlement brings a sense of relief. This guide provides valuable insights into how disputes can be avoided altogether, and Mediation used earlier, so that time, money and energy are not wasted in pursuing goals which will also damage human relationships. The message of the guide could not be more timely."

Mark Jackson-Stops, Head of Chambers, IPOS Mediation.

"This book is 'classic Richbell' – practical, encouraging and very human. It is also a wonderful tribute to my dear friend David, whose son Olly clearly carries the family torch for humane and real dispute resolution."

Bill Marsh, Independent Mediator and Who's Who Legal Mediator of the Year in 2023.

The Dispute Avoidance & Resolution Partnership team have designed and written a series of courses and workshops on Dispute Avoidance, Dispute Management and Dispute Resolution which set the basis for this Guide. Each course and workshop can be tailored to meet any specific need and if you would wish to discuss how they can delivered to your business please contact us via office@thedarp.co.uk or on 01234 241 242.

CONTENTS

INTRODUCTION

The Dispute Avoidance & Resolution Partnership ("The DARP") provides Volcano Insurance through a range of services to help its clients avoid, manage and resolve disputes quickly, efficiently and cost effectively.

The work to bring this Guide together was initially led by David Richbell who was at the forefront of the first Mediation revolution in the early 1990's. David began mediating commercial disputes in 1992 and mediated in excess of 1,000 cases. He was passionate about the need for there to be a positive alternative to the devasting trench warfare of litigation, and a positive (even restorative) way of resolving conflict in business and in society in general. In May 2015 Oliver, having spent years as a commercial litigator and David formed The DARP with David Evans, Ian White, Stephen Hall, Wolf von Kumberg and Zaza Johnson-Elsheikh joining as Consultants.

The overriding factor that binds all the contributors together in this Guide is the shared belief that a second revolution is required in how disputes are avoided, managed and resolved. The DARP passionately believes that a greater focus on communication and relationship building will help effective Dispute Avoidance, risk management and the resolution of conflict wherever it may arise.

This Guide delivers the experience, wisdom and aspirations of seven people who spend most of their time advising, guiding and rescuing businesses and individuals that get into, or are heading for disputes. This Guide is not just aimed at businesses or individuals as charities, faith communities and not-for-profit organisations are all included in our collective experiences and in this Guide we use "business" to encapsulate all types of organisations from sole managers to international conglomerates, and every size in between. From boardrooms and partnerships to factory floors our combined knowledge has helped businesses work better by avoiding conflict, by effectively managing conflict when it arises and by settling issues when they escalate to disputes.

The aim of this Guide

The main objective is to help leaders in society, in business, in government and or in the public sector (particularly those in positions of authority and responsibility) to operate their businesses better and more effectively thereby saving both time and money.

The Guide will also assist leaders (but indeed anyone that is in a dispute or conflict situation) to learn and develop from our collective experiences and to help strengthen existing skills for dealing with difficult situations and sharpen instincts and heighten awareness in order to avoid disputes and conflict from occurring in the first place.

All the contributors to this Guide are either trained and or practising Mediators, negotiators and or facilitators, so we all have first-hand experience of what happens when things go wrong and how difficulties can so easily escalate into disputes.

We can reflect on every Mediation or negotiation and recognise that "if only x had said that (or not said that) or done that (or not done that) then, they wouldn't have needed us".

The DARP want to apply the principles of Mediation, facilitation and collaboration as early as possible in everyday business situations in order to prevent disputes and conflict arising.

Why have Volcano Insurance

It would be easy to suggest that The DARP and this Guide is offering a service that no-one needs because *"I always get what I want"* or *"No need for Mediation or Dispute Resolution consultants because my business has never had a dispute"*. However, the uncertain and challenging times of the first two decades of the twenty-first century highlights the relevance and practicality of this Guide.

So *"Why pay for an insurance policy that I'll never need?"* The answer is simple; when the dispute event occurs, the conflict arises or to put it another way the volcano erupts the immediate reaction is to exacerbate the situation by making statements like *"See you in court"* or *"I'll put this in the hands of my lawyers"* or other such acerbic assertions. These tend to only position parties where they have no choice but to incur vast legal costs and such widens, often terminally, the dispute or issue thereby reducing the chances of any proportionate and timely outcome being achieved.

Like most types of insurance the benefit is only ever experienced when the worst has happened and that is the absolute notion of Volcano Insurance *"We've never had a volcano erupt – We could be about due then"*.

No-one wants to be in dispute or to operate under conflict as this is not good for business. The DARP do not believe that businesses or individuals want to spend their valuable time arguing or to expend more time and effort on disputes and especially not to allow financial resources to be depleted on the unknown costs of litigation. However, conflict, risk and dispute occur on a daily basis and this Guide sets out the Volcano Insurance protection that provides the benefit of hindsight beforehand.

Why this Guide is important?

So much of this Guide is about effective communication within relationships. We are living in an age where personal contact (i.e. face-to-face) is becoming increasingly rarer as the written word prevails and where videoconferencing, texts, emails and social media dominate as the preferred method of communication, the risks of miscommunication and the creation of fractured relationships has risen sharply. With the greater impact that Artificial Intelligence will have on the way communication occurs in the future the potential for greater miscommunication is exacerbated.

The written word, with no expression, pace or emphasis to relay its meaning, is often a dangerous tool. It is the least effective method of communicating both from conveying the message but also from building an effective relationship.

When relationships are solid and trust has been built, issues are more likely to be dealt with co-operatively and a dispute avoided. When relationships are not positive, and so trust is not present, attitudes become defensive and adversarial and an issue that could have been avoided descends into a dispute and that is good for the lawyers but very bad for business whereas this Guide is good for business.

PART 1

Avoiding Disputes

In order to avoid disputes there has to be a realisation that effective communication and relationships are integral components for the successful avoidance of disputes as ineffective communication or even different communication styles create confusion, disharmony, distrust and even resentment and these can only ever lead to future issues, conflict and disputes.

To actually avoid disagreements, issues or differences of opinion escalating into disputes there is a fundamental need to communicate effectively. There is a necessity, when negotiating, that the positions and final contracts accurately reflect the party's positions and also provide the appropriate mechanism for the avoidance of litigation. There is also a need to ensure that there is sufficient capacity to recognise a dispute, identify conflict and have in place a bespoke process to achieve the avoidance of disputes.

Dispute Avoidance is best for business as it is the most cost effective way of dealing with disputes and the DARP's message is always that the best way to resolve a dispute is to avoid it in the first place.

Communication & Relationships
Effective communications in relationships

It was George Bernard Shaw who remarked *"The single biggest problem in communication is the illusion that it has taken place"*.

Most people in business and in life can generally recognise the signs of growing conflict such as talking at each other (instead of listening to each other), the use of ever more emotive and exaggerated language to describe problems and wants, the upping the ante in the positions taken and the adoption of the 'victim mentality'.

Given that the best outcome in any situation which could develop into a dispute is for the parties to work at managing disagreements before they become disputes, there are a number of actions an individual party can take to stop the escalation process and actively avoid the issue descending into a dispute. These should be approaches that good leaders, in any organisation, operate every day because, ultimately, effective communication is everything in business.

In this part of the Guide we look at approaches and techniques to manage disagreements to a successful outcome and avoid a deterioration into the entrenched positions of a dispute.

Effective communication

Most issues, disputes, legal battles (and indeed many wars) have arisen because of ineffective communication and non-communication. Failure to communicate effectively means that the message, stance or opinion of you or your business is not being received by the intended recipient. As a consequence communication breaks down and that is the precursor to issues, disputes, legal battles and even wars developing.

There are a number of actions a party can take to improve communication.

Make time:

Not all conversations can be planned, so making time to do the conversation justice may not be easy. Planning means making enough time (i.e. as long as is needed), finding the right place (away from distractions and interruptions) and creating the right atmosphere (relaxed and, if possible, neutral). If that is possible, then great, it should be a fruitful conversation. Where this is not possible, then do not feel pressurised into a rushed and unprepared conversation and communicate the need for more time openly and not combatively. Also try not to rise to the bait and always avoid an instant reaction so also make time to give an attentive response.

Empathy, empathy and then empathy:

Empathy simply means 'walking in the shoes of another' and to see issues as the other party sees them. The most powerful way to find a solution to an issue which is causing disagreement is to truly put yourself in the shoes of the other aggrieved party. If you can visualise their issue, then you can feel the emotion which the other feels. Demonstrating empathy can be as simple as thinking about how you would feel if the positions were reversed before you say anything and or to think how you would feel if someone said it to you or acted in such a way to you. Every person and business are different and what might seem fair or reasonable to you or your company might not be taken as so by the recipient and therefore take a moment for empathy and consideration and the outcome will be the better for it.

Being empathetic doesn't mean being sympathetic by any means it just means envisaging what the other party needs to put matters right and having the courage to take that action. Imagine what you would want by way of a solution if you had the same problem or what would a good solution look like from the other party's perspective, and how could you propose a solution which then assists them but also helps you.

Hearing:

People need to feel heard. Hearing is subtly different to listening. So many people listen in part but are more focused on how they are going to reply or they are more concerned with their own thoughts and story than the one being voiced.

When someone feels heard, they feel valued and that makes a huge difference to the natural frustration that arises from knowing that the listener is distracted or not giving proper attention to what is being said.

However, hearing is only part of the process. The hearer must show that what has been said has been understood. The best way of doing that is to summarise what has been said, which has the dual advantage of showing that the speaker has been heard, and that the key points have been understood. Summarising also allows the speaker to correct or reframe what is being fed back if they do not agree.

Summarising:

Summarising is an instrumental method of:
- checking understanding
- demonstrating that the listener has heard what has been said
- focussing on key issues
- allowing parties to change or clarify what they have said
- putting order into an otherwise disordered statement
- reframing a negative statement
- changing the direction of a conversation and
- buying time, both for the party to reflect and also for the listener to reflect

It is particularly important not to move on from summarising until the party has said 'Yes' or indicated agreement. Waiting for confirmation allows the speaker to review what has been said and then to adjust the emphasis or interpretation.

Active listening:

Being a good listener implies not talking (very much) and it means being prepared to listen to what the other person has to say without interrupting or taking over the conversation even when what the speaker is saying is emotive, combative or argumentative.

As mentioned above, active listening also means hearing what is being said and demonstrating that you have heard the speaker. It additionally means leaving silence, and not filling the space, but perhaps more importantly encouraging the other person to carry on by giving a few gentle prompts. There are subtle ways of demonstrating that what is being said is being heard without actually saying anything. Minimal prompts such as 'Mmm…', and 'Uh-ha…', will encourage the speaker to continue. When the flow falters then 'Tell me more about…', or 'Could you please expand on' will encourage the flow. A raising of the eyebrows (as opposed to rolling of the eyes) or gesture of the hands can also invite more. Or just in some cases silence.

Active listening furthermore means not bettering their story with one of your own or talking over the speaker and most certainly not indicating that the listener has not valued what they have heard from the speaker by shaking of heads, tutting, laughing, fidgeting or just plain old gazing into the distance. It is all too common for the listener to try and disregard what they have heard with their own narrative and sometimes this is undertaken as an attempt to demonstrate empathy with a similar story or event but it actually has a wholly counter-productive reaction as the original speaker will often feel that their voice and words have been disregarded and overlooked.

It is not easy being a good listener and it takes time and patience too which is why it is crucially important that the conversation is not rushed, unplanned or undertaken in an unsuitable location such as communal office areas, public transport or in front of peers.

Questioning appropriately:

There are other skills used by a listener that can also have a considerable effect on the course and indeed outcome of a conversation. The style and method of questioning, the ability to challenge without appearing to be critical, being deeply interested without being inquisitorial, reframing negative or adversarial statements into positive, more conciliatory words, all of these can be fundamental to helping the speaker to move on. The wrong questions can risk blocking communication and even devastate rapport. It is a very true adage that a positive environment can take time to develop but can be lost rapidly.

Of course, different types of questions can be effective at different times, but some types of questions are rarely helpful in a difficult conversation. These include *leading* questions where the questioner indicates the expected answer, and *multiple* questions where the questioner asks the same question in several different ways and unnecessarily confuses the listener.

The easiest way of gathering information and encouraging someone to speak is by using *open* questions. Questions that start 'How….?' or 'What…..?' or 'Why…?' or 'Tell me more about….' invite the listener to speak at length, whereas closed questions invite a 'Yes' or 'No' answer that provide little or no information, context or scope for the conversation to continue.

It is common that closed questions are used more instinctively but often it is just a matter of reordering the words to change a closed question into an open one. For example: 'Are you OK about that?'

(= 'Yes' or 'No') could be 'Tell me how you feel about that?' or 'how did that make you feel?'

There are times when closed questions are appropriate, particularly to obtain confirmation of understanding but they are not appropriate for encouraging people to speak.

The use of *hypothetical* ('What if....?') questions is a powerful technique when exploring possible ideas without anyone taking responsibility. It depersonalises the suggestion and allows it to be examined dispassionately without emotion clouding the answer.

Challenging questions can be used to great effect, particularly when reality-testing. 'Why...?' is one of the best. The challenge, however, is to be sure that the questions are worded so as not to imply criticism or judgement of the other person's position. Alternatively, you can try and soften a 'Why...?' question with a different question such as, 'What is it that you think should happen next?'.

Ensuring understanding:

In the heightened environment of emerging disagreement it is important to go beyond making the other party understand.

Dr John Lund put it succinctly: *"Don`t communicate to be understood; rather, communicate so as not to be misunderstood."*

If this means asking more clarifying questions and summarising again then do this to avoid misunderstanding. This is increasingly important in professional life today where much more global business is taking place and more and more communication is via online platforms and videoconferences. Factor in again that English may not be a first language as well so a person's particular use of language may not be as precise as yours, so assume positive intent and clarify.

Non-verbal communication:

Non-verbal is what it says – we communicate with much more than words however unfortunately in the digital age, we rely on the written word much more and it is fraught with the danger of being misunderstood. The written word has the meaning received by the recipient, rather than the meaning of the sender, and they may not necessarily be the same and without explanation or seeking clarity of understanding the meaning is entirely how the receiver interprets the words. How much more meaningful then are words that have expression, tone, volume and pace to accompany them – telephone conversations are a much better means of conveying the true meaning of the words and also such enables the speaker to explain further if the listener has misunderstood or seeks clarification.

Even then, communication is incomplete. Face-to-face communication is so much more effective. People, when face-to-face, can see expression, have eye contact (or not), read body language, interpret inconsistencies between posture and words, cease to demonise the other person and recognise that they are also human with feelings and needs.

Part of building rapport is being in harmony with a person. A person can enhance that by *matching* another person's body language. That does not mean mimicking or appearing to parody – harmony is the key word. When a group of friends are sitting together, relaxed and at ease with each other, their body posture is often the same. Legs crossed, sitting back, arms moving when they talk. Unconsciously they are *matching* and being in harmony with each other. So it is with rapport-building, having a body posture that is consistent with the other person, subtly matching their pace and tone of voice and using key words that they have used all helps the person to relax and feel valued. But 'subtle' is the word; more than that and it could be taken as artificial or insulting.

There is potentially a place for *mismatching* although this does come with a strong health warning. Bringing a ranting monologue or a meeting to end by standing up, raising your volume and emotion, or by looking at your watch, phone or clock can occasionally break down barriers and bring an end to bellicose dialogue but the danger is that all the careful rapport-building that has gone before may be undone in an instant.

Managing emotion:

One 'rule' of effective communication is that if someone is becoming emotional, DON'T sit on it and DON'T avoid it. If they are stopped from expressing their emotion a head of steam can build up that could dramatically adversely affect the conversation and its outcome. If emotion is avoided, because it is uncomfortable (who for?) the same will happen, with the emotional person left wondering if they have been ignored or undervalued or that they have been unfairly categorised as a difficult or combative person.

There is no better way to build rapport with someone than to let them freely vent their emotion, and then to acknowledge and value (which does not mean agreement) what has been said. It can be scary; ultimately however, working with another's emotions may allow you to help them explore what might be needed for them to move towards a solution in the midst of a difficult or conflict situation. The danger is that strong emotion can fuel itself and become overwhelming to all concerned. The temptation then is to intervene but first ask the question 'Why?' If it is just because people are feeling uncomfortable then it may be worth letting it run until it fades away. However, if it becomes abusive or pugnacious then intervention is of course necessary, so long as it is done without demeaning the speaker and with an acknowledgement of their strong feeling. Saying things like "Pull yourself together" or "I think you're being overly dramatic" are not going to be constructive responses!

Conclusion:

Focusing on good communication and building relationships is critical to avoiding disputes and delivering success in business. Most disputes arise because of ineffective communication or non-communication, and there are a number of actions a party can take to improve communication. Of these showing empathy (walking in the shoes of another) to see issues as the other party sees them, is the most powerful way to find a solution to an issue. This, together with a range of techniques to ensure we listen to and question others can make a positive difference to ensure the dispute is avoided, conflict does not arise, or is resolved as early as possible after it arises.

Having difficult conversations

One of the most difficult challenges in modern society seems to be having, and in particular, starting a difficult conversation.

It is a natural human instinct to shy away from the potential discomfort of confronting another person with our unhappiness, point of dispute or general disagreement probably fearing that the situation could exacerbate or permanently fracture an already challenged relationship. However and almost inevitably, if the matter is not raised, it will fester and become a much more challenging problem in the future. Therefore a much more difficult conversation is required and consequently a mutual resolution will be much harder to find.

Doing nothing resolves nothing. At best it just fades into a distant, unsatisfactory past, with the likely potential of resentment and resurrection in the future.

What is conversation?

Conversation is a two-way exchange between two or more people and happens on several levels. In general, the intention is to impart information and that information is conveyed, coloured and reinforced by volume, tone and pace of voice and by posture, gesture and expression of body. Hence face-to-face communication is much more effective than writing (where only words convey the message and can hardly be termed a conversation) or even via telephone (where the voice conveys the message but the body doesn't).

In the 1960s, Professor Albert Mehrabian's initial research and analysis of effective communication suggested that:

The words we use accounts for 7% of the meaning conveyed. Therefore just writing them is the least efficient.

The voice (tone, pitch, volume, inflection) accounts for 38% of the meaning conveyed. So therefore speaking them is more efficient than writing them.

Face-to-face communication (body language, posture, gesture, voice and words) accounts for 55% of the meaning conveyed. So face-to-face has the chance of turning words into 100% effective communication.

Quite apart from the voice and body, other forces impact on a conversation:

- Emotion
- History
- Self-perception

Firstly, it is a fact that we all have emotion and some of it is negative. Some people show emotion more readily than others but we all have it and it affects the way we communicate whether we think it does or not. Our inner self is projected through how we give the message, through tone, expression, pace and the words we use will reflect our mood, be it positive or negative, disinterested or enthusiastic. All of these affect the way a message is given, received and interpreted.

Secondly, it is also affected by history. Our own history and the history of our relationship (if any) with the person, business, or group, with whom we are communicating. Our own history because we will have conscious or unconscious bias formed through our life experiences and personality. Whether or not we know the person, or group, with whom we are communicating we cannot enter a conversation in a totally neutral and unbiased way. We make assumptions (consciously and sub-consciously) based upon our history and influenced by our own self-perception.

Thirdly, our self-perception impacts on a conversation. How we feel about ourselves, our level of self-worth and our confidence both in ourselves and in the message that we are intending to communicate. What does this problem say about me? Am I a successful business person or intelligent person, a good person, worthy of love? That will show through in the image projected and the sort of conversation that will ultimately take place.

Preparing for a difficult conversation

Have the courage:

Realising that a difficult conversation is needed does not make it happen. It takes courage, and a risk of feeling vulnerable, to initiate the process. The fact is that almost always the problem will only get worse if it is ignored or put off. Rarely do situations improve by doing nothing or prevaricating. So the earlier a problem is addressed, the easier the solution is likely to be.

Getting started:

How can the conversation be initiated in a way that a request to have one receives a positive response? It is obviously key that the request for a conversation is inviting and not overtly threatening or passive aggressive. It is best kept brief (there can always be a follow-up) and ideally suggests a reasonable date, time and venue. The question, whether the invitation is written or verbal, is how much information should be relayed within it? Should the reason be included? Generally, yes but not in great detail. Should the word 'confidential' be mentioned? Generally yes, but it could cause concern. There is a danger of being too careful but this is part of a difficult conversation and getting started is just part of the difficulty.

Defining the headline:

In any commercial negotiation the starting point is getting the headline agreed; what is the reason for the conversation and what is the desired outcome. By setting the headline this means that everyone should be focussed on the same thing. This establishes the touchpoint and the reference for the ensuing conversation. It helps to keep the conversation focussed and provide a necessary base and purpose for it as well.

Rehearse, especially the opening:

Before going into the difficult conversation, it is always worth rehearsing, especially the first few words as they set the scene and it is therefore prudent to take time getting them right. If you are the 'injured' party it will be very tempting to be aggressive, but that will, more than likely, result in a defensive response. To get the best out of the conversation, the opening needs to be conciliatory, welcoming, recognising a mutual problem and seeking a mutual solution. This is not about winning (or losing), although there is a good chance that the outcome will be a win for both people. So the tone, and the outcome, will be set by the opening words. By preparing and taking time over the opening words will help structure the conversation and set the groundwork to achieve a positive outcome.

Face the demon, forget the blame:

So often a person having a disagreement demonises the other and this person becomes the sole reason for their current misfortune; sometimes even for all their misfortune. Although it is often resisted, having people in the same room together bursts the demon balloon and makes them see the other as a fellow human-being with feelings and emotions of their own. 'Popping the demon' is an essential step in helping people find a co-operative approach to the subject matter of the difficult conversation. The problem is that many people actually like to have a 'demon' onto which they can focus their resentment, dissatisfaction and even vitriol (and this even enables people to be nice to everyone else) and that can be difficult to let go of but it is pure self-indulgence.

Modern day is sadly though a blame culture – something happens, someone is to blame and they must pay. Shaking that off and seeing the problem as being a problem for everyone, and that the best solution will be reached mutually, is a big step towards having a successful conversation.

Saving face (yours and theirs):

Face is not just a cultural issue; it is an intensely personal one and intertwined with a person's feeling of dignity and self- worth. People need to avoid losing face and, to bring a difficult conversation to an end, that means they can leave with their 'head high'. One person's need to crush the other, or for revenge, or to be seen to 'win', needs to be replaced by the recognition that the best outcomes come from co-operation and meeting the other's needs. Finding solutions that preserve people's dignity means that there is no residual resentment or anger and therefore relationships can be saved and even repaired and the potential for further time (and therefore money) to be expended on repeating the difficult conversation again in the future is minimised.

Look to the future, not back at the past:

The sad fact is you can't change the past, and that's where a lot of people in dispute or a legal battle are rooted. However you can influence and control the future.

There comes a time when looking back at the history needs to change to looking ahead towards how this may be resolved for the better. Most people know they have to let go of the past – it is done, out of their control and to be learned from – and often a reason is needed to turn and face the future.

End positively:

The best outcome of the conversation is that the people involved feel better informed, that they understand what has driven the other side to the position they are in, and that they are able to move on to start shaping an outcome.

Even if that is not the result, then the likelihood is that the deliverer will have removed a blockage and can move on to more positive things in the future, and the receiver, whilst not being able to accept what has been said, at least understands the problem and the reason for the conversation.

The worst outcome would be for the conversation to backfire, be badly delivered and badly received which could end the entire conversation and prevent any positive outcome and inhibit an effective relationship in the future.

During a difficult conversation look out for and avoid:

look out for:

- Inconsistencies from both deliverer and receiver in words, expression and body language. That will challenge the authenticity of what is being said
- Switching off by the receiver, and, even more importantly, the deliverer when receiving a response
- Hints or markers that suggest underlying issues that have not been revealed

and avoid:

- Pointing out the other's mistakes. The fact is they, and history, can't be changed. However, at the end it could be appropriate to ask what lessons had been learned that means they won't be back having another difficult conversation again

- Expecting forgiveness. It may be that the disagreement has been sorted, a settlement achieved, a future seen without conflict, everyone moving on, learning from the problems and even forgiving each other but do not expect it.

Conclusion:

It may be that using an independent person to facilitate a difficult conversation would make the conversation more possible. It could be a trusted colleague or someone completely from the 'outside'. That person would be in an incredibly important, and powerful position, in conducting or facilitating a difficult conversation, so that person needs to be carefully chosen and ideally mutually. But chosen well, by retelling their stories in a way that is true for both at the same time, by reframing, by summarising, by modelling their behaviour, a trusted independent person can transform a situation of high conflict to one of understanding and co-operation. It is a big responsibility but one that can bring tangible rewards and a real privilege to be able to transform a difficult conversation into productive dialogue.

Conflict can be positive

The word 'conflict' tends to create a negative reaction in people. It is something to be avoided and can even be a sign of failure or discomfort. But actually conflict can be a catalyst for change, for innovation, for learning, understanding and developing.

Psychology of conflict - The physical reasons:

A part of our brain – the amygdala – inherits our ancestors' primitive reaction to danger. It overrides the logical part of our brain to give an immediate, rather than a delayed rational response. It is the fight, flight or freeze part and it still kicks in when we feel threatened, whether it be physical or our integrity or our self-esteem is questioned. The challenge is to develop strategies to combat it and turn it into a positive and dynamic influence.

Psychology of conflict - The emotional reasons:

Aside from the instinctive reactions to conflict there are other reasons which cause otherwise rational people, to squander time, money, energy and emotion on protracted warfare. It usually bears no relationship to common sense but is all to do with self-worth and our modern day blame culture (something happens, someone is to blame and they must pay) just fuels it. When parties, people or businesses are in conflict they rarely act rationally for they are more likely to be driven by emotion and often they are not aware of their underlying emotions. So when conflict occurs and it is perceived as a threat, the defence mechanisms kick in and the emotional response prevails. An allegation of 'fault' (and therefore 'blame') or negligence often creates strong feelings of hurt, resentment and anger and when they are denied, the accuser in turn is likely to feel offended as insult has now been added to injury.

Psychology of conflict - The cultural reasons:

'Culture' does not mean other nationalities or people with different ethnicity. It means 'This is how we do it here'. We all live in a culture formed by our family and friends and the wider community in which we live and of course the company or organisation that we work for or lead. We inherit values which form the principles by which we live and which give us boundaries for an 'ordered' life. It must be no surprise then that we become challenged when another person lives by different, or no, values.

The need to be heard:

Many of the belligerent clashes around the world today are the result of people or nations feeling that their voice is not being heard.

A wish to speak to others about matters that are of importance to them can deteriorate into more forceful protest and their voices get louder and louder. Still unheard or ignored, shouting and peaceful remonstration descend into violence and eventually war.

When it is felt that your voice or your opinion is not valued, being valued does not mean agreed with, the more than likely outcome is that there is exacerbation not de-escalation. The need to be heard is part of basic human instinct and denying this also leads to resentment, dis-engagement and sometimes even a desire for future retribution.

Find space:

Finding space to turn threats into opportunities is crucial. Conflict and co-operation need not be separate, but rather they can be phases of the same process. The first thing is to recognise that our instinctive, and emotional, response is not necessarily the best and also it is imperative that others might have their own separate instinctive and emotional responses. Wanting to run, or confront, or freeze until the danger passes may be appropriate sometimes, but, whatever the reaction, taking a deep breath and pausing to reflect on the opportunity that this conflict may bring, could bring far greater rewards.

Conflict can bring new ideas, can be the catalyst for innovation, can lead to discovery and greater knowledge. Conflict can be positive, and the way to make it positive is to take time and be prepared to:

- Listen
- Understand
- Value
- Co-operate

As mentioned in many places in this Guide, listening is a key and enriching skill. People want to be heard and giving time and demonstrating that they are being heard is the key to everything else. It leads to understanding, valuing and eventually to co-operating in working out a solution. Co-operative solutions last, because they are jointly sought, worked out and owned whereas imposed solutions (for example court judgments) are, for one side, often challenged, more than often resented and almost inevitably the beginning of placing blame.

The key is that first moment when confronted with conflict and that first reaction can be the difference between a negative and destructive act or one that is positive and productive.

Non-judgemental acceptance:

In a world where judgement and punishment are the norm, accepting difference, whether that be in opinion or in person, is a vital part of meaningful communication. It is another part of being human to have your own opinions and thoughts and observations but not negatively reacting to them when someone has a different opinion, thought or observation will only have a positive difference in ensuring that the communication continues effectively. It is not easy by any means and it takes time but an essential part of effective communication is to embrace non-judgemental acceptance.

Different truths:

The truth is that people see the same facts and events through different eyes and due to a whole lot of reasons (education, culture, ethnicity, wealth, politics and also as a result of the advice they have received). They may be right, but another person who interprets them differently may also be right. And as time passes, each other's different truths become more certain and polarised so that one party sees the other as offensively distorting the truth to suit their own ends. Only by being prepared to talk about the differences and to recognise that other views are genuinely held, will the barriers be dismantled.

There is passion in asserting that 'this is the truth' but it is actually 'your truth' not necessarily the truth and part of accepting that conflict can be positive is also accepting that different truths exist and in order to continue to communicate effectively and to avoid disputes there is a fundamental need to discuss the differing versions of each sides truths.

Separating people from the problem:

Facts and emotions often get mixed up and unravelling them can be the key to addressing a problem and avoiding a dispute. Helping people to isolate the facts (this is the problem) and to recognise that we all bring our emotions into situations of conflict (the people part), and so deal with the two aspects separately, can bring clarity and understanding to the situation. The fundamental process is to identify the facts, identify the emotion. Work on the former, accept and value the latter.

Conclusion:

Whilst it is always the calmer option to move away from a conflict situation there needs to be an acceptance that conflict can be positive or perhaps to put it another way positive conflict can be beneficial if understood, delivered and managed appropriately. Easier written than done for certain but sometimes embracing the conflict situation is the archetypical short-term pain long-term gain situation.

How to Avoid Disputes

Complaints handling

While Mediation should not be a last resort, there are many stages that precede it which, if undertaken successfully, will mean that Mediation is never actually required. As has been highlighted above, good communication is one but another equally valid resource is good complaints handling. Having a good policy in this area, whether it is for customers, employees or other stakeholders can go a long way to ensure you never have to pick up the phone to the Mediator or attend a Mediation. And when it comes to customers, it is vastly more prohibitive both in terms of time and cost to acquire a new customer than it is to retain an existing one.

So what does a good complaints handling process entail?

- First, it needs to be straightforward and easy to follow. If it does not meet these two cardinal rules, then it will fail from the very beginning. Complaints are stressful for all concerned but particularly the person making the complaint. They are an unhappy customer and emotions are riding high. They want to be able to quickly outline what has gone wrong and know the procedure for finding a resolution. If it is complex, the issue will escalate, the process will fail and there will be recourse to more costly resolution methods. If you work within a regulated sector, there may even be a regulatory requirement to follow a set straightforward procedure

- Second, it must be clearly communicated. People need to know how to complain but if there is no easy way to find out how to do so then the issue will escalate (even if the process for escalation is not clear!). It is amazing the number of company websites that have their complaints procedure hidden somewhere obscure. We have already talked about the importance of good communication and so you should follow the principles there. In essence, make sure in all your dealings with customers and staff that they can complain, that the process is straightforward for doing so and the name of the person to contact is readily available

- Third, any process must be followed. However tempting, do not create a process and then forget to follow it. You would be surprised how many organisations fall foul of this. If you are dealing with a workplace issue a failure to follow procedure could, of course, be fatal to any issue no matter how meritorious your defence of it is. This is another reason why it helps to have a straightforward procedure that everyone can easily follow and evidence that this is the case

- Fourth, any complaints process should contain a degree of independence. For some complaints, it may be necessary for the customer to deal with the person who was their original contact and whom the compliant was about. However, if the issue cannot be resolved this way, then it needs to be handed to someone who is completely independent. Depending on the nature and gravity of the issue, this may even be someone outside the organisation who can look at the matter completely objectively without fear or favour

- Fifth, it must be handled fairly. If you follow the principles above, then that should be the natural conclusion. However, and this is the reason for having someone independent looking at the complaint, if you are irritated by what the complainant has instigated then there is always the risk that you will not deal with the matter fairly. So be clear when it is appropriate to get an independent resource to help you

- Sixth, if you can reach agreement over the complaint, set out in a brief document how it has been resolved and get everyone to sign up to their agreement about what this says. This isn't a legally binding agreement but it does help evidence that the matter was resolved in case it occurs again. And, of course, it provides a useful precedent of how you deal with complaints

- Finally, for staff complaints there needs to be a culture of openness that encourages staff to raise issues without fear of reprisals. This goes to the heart of the company culture where staff feel supported and where a blame culture is discouraged.

Conclusion:

If you have followed the process above then hopefully the complaint will have been resolved to the satisfaction of all parties and recourse to other options will not be required.

Drafting Contracts & escalating Dispute Resolution clauses

Contract drafting is an art form, those that are good at it regard themselves as akin to Turner; those that are not fall back on the Turner prize idiom of *'I don't get it'*.

A well drafted and structured commercial contract is the cornerstone of modern business. Without a contract or set of terms and conditions that are *'fit for purpose'* and of *'satisfactory quality'* the scope and propensity for issues to arise and disputes is immense; it's perhaps even more alarming than that as it is probable and not just possible that parties to a poorly drafted contract or set of terms and conditions will be involved in disagreements and litigation before their commercial relationship concludes.

Getting it right from the start:

Engagement is everything. Engagement means far more than just communication. The engagement of the parties as well as their advisors from the outset should, through effective communication in relationships and if need be by negotiating intelligently, lead naturally to a finalised agreement that reflects, in a more balanced fashion, the commercial intentions and needs of the parties.

If the parties or stakeholders are not actively engaged in the determination of the written agreement and it is left to advisors or lawyers there is a danger that the final form presented for signing does not reflect the actual aims of the commercial purpose; it could even be the case that what is prepared, whilst correct in law is utterly at odds with what was expected. This eventuality is perhaps most likely to occur when one party is unrepresented and has, with the belief that it would be more cost effective for them, allowed the other side's legal team to prepare the documentation.

It is worth noting that there will not always exist an equality of bargaining positions between the parties who are negotiating or preparing a contract; for example in a construction scenario a sub-contractor is often likely to have more adverse terms imposed on them by a contractor and in turn the contractor may well have terms imposed on them by the employer. In this type of situation where it is less of a 'buy/sell' or 'payment for services' transaction the engagement of parties in the drafting, formation, amending, negotiating and finalisation of the contract or terms and conditions is crucial in order to avoid the occurrence of future disputes and or litigation.

Bespoke or template:

There is no settled school of thought on whether it is better to use template agreements or to draft from scratch save to advance the obvious that the use of templates would have originally started with a blank sheet of paper.

Much of what the parties actually need is infinitesimal compared to what advisors assert is paramount to include however there is little doubt that a contract, agreement or set of terms and conditions are going to be more detailed and more robust if they have been drafted by lawyers. It would also be accurate to advance the point that agreements that have been prepared and signed without legal input and or advice can often lead to disputes over interpretation and design far more quickly. However the parties to the contracts are more important than the lawyers and the latter group need to realise this and ensure that the paying client is actually fully involved in the preparation and drafting stage rather than kept in the dark and only involved right at the end.

All agreements require careful deliberation. It is neither prudent in terms of commerce nor law, to expect one contract to be a perfect fit for another, even if it appears to be identical. It is also not sensible commercial practice to sign a contract without first understanding it, but both of these occur regularly and cause parties to become involved in disputes that could have, and should have, been avoided.

It is an accepted tradition that the 'boilerplate' clauses (the set of non-operative provisions) are often drafted and reviewed as standard and although in principle there is nothing obviously wrong with accepting the items to be included, the reliance on standard drafts is rarely a productive mechanism for an effective and commercially successful relationship.

A can of worms over a minefield:

It could easily be argued that a party who accepts the other-side's standard terms and conditions in order to avoid opening the preverbal 'can of worms' does so at their own peril. Many businesses want to avoid the legal minefield of contractual debate and the 'travelling draft' however the simple reality of the situation is that accepting any terms without review or consideration may lead to a sense of injustice because they are seen to be one-sided, which will tend to only expedite the escalation of disputes.

It is easy to be wistfully reflective with hindsight propounding how unfair and how staggered you are when terms or conditions signed and accepted are utilised to one party's disadvantage. Court rooms are filled with parties demanding 'justice' and 'fairness' but these equitable outcomes are not always going to be possible as the courts have declared it is not their responsibility to protect commercial parties from a bad bargain.

Prevention is preferable:

It is in everyone's long term interests if parties work together in a collaborative and open way with regards to the formalisation of contractual terms. There will always be occasions during such discussions and negotiations where elements of disagreement occur but it is important to hold onto the fact that conflict can be positive provided that it is approached in a pragmatic way. It is also imperative that lawyers do not engage in the overly tired and all too typical game of trying to 'beat' their opponent as in the end it is only the paying clients that suffer as costs inevitably increase and at times the deal can even fall through as a result of excessive battles over the minutiae of the draft contract.

Multi-tiered Dispute Resolution clauses:

It is rare that parties to a commercial transaction or lawyers representing their clients will be engaged in much debate over the boilerplate provisions however the inclusion of a robust and bespoke escalating Dispute Resolution clause can operate as a 'fail-safe' mechanism in the event that a dispute emerges after the contract has been entered into. The advantages to such an inclusion are that the parties can engage in a pre-agreed set of processes to deal with any issues in a cost effective and time efficient way thereby keeping the parties focused on their operative obligations under the agreement.

Dispute Resolution clauses:

The basic principle behind Dispute Resolution is to resolve disputes. That bit should not be overly contentious but the how, why and when of it often gets the parties, lawyers and academics into a frenzied state of uproar often blinding them to the ironic absurdity of disputing Dispute Resolution.

It should be an accepted mandatory requirement of all commercial agreements and contracts that a Dispute Resolution clause is included. However it is not.

Moreover it is also often the case that the reliance on a 'boilerplate' Dispute Resolution clause actually has no practical benefit, for example a clause that propounds the use of Arbitration, but the contractual quantum is of a minor amount to make Arbitration utterly prohibitive, is not an effective Dispute Resolution clause. Furthermore a construction contract that only refers to the Adjudication of disputes has palpably overlooked that Adjudication is a right under statute and therefore applied by law into the agreement.

It is therefore of paramount importance that the parties work together on the careful and suitable wording of the Dispute Resolution clause to make sure that it is *'fit for purpose'* and will bind the parties to agree to it in the event that a dispute or disagreement arises under the over-arching agreement.

Escalating Dispute Resolution clauses in commercial agreements:

In larger scale projects or contracts it is common to use escalating Dispute Resolution clauses, which are sometimes referred to as multi-tiered or stepped Dispute Resolution clauses. The Spectrum of available Dispute Resolution processes is included at the start of Part 3 (Resolving Disputes) of this Guide.

In basic terms an escalating Dispute Resolution clause provides the parties to an agreement with a structured process of addressing any dispute or disagreement that emerges on a step-by-step basis. If it is drafted well and tailored to the parties' needs and the transaction itself then it should be able to effectively deal with any situation that may arise under the contract. Most Dispute Resolution steps in contracts are:

- Local
- Executive
- 3rd party
- Determination
- Imposed

Local resolution requires those people involved in the dispute to co-operatively resolve the situation themselves.

Executive resolution involves a higher level of management, not usually involved in the contract, on each side attempting to negotiate a settlement. It would be normal and possibly more effective if, at this initial stage, the parties didn't involve solicitors as it might be that the stakeholders could resolve any issue on a commercial not legal basis. Although if lawyers had been involved in the drafting of the over-arching contract and the escalating Dispute Resolution clause it could be that their collective involvement could be beneficial and this is of assistance in resolving any dispute at this initial stage provided of course that those lawyers actually want to help resolve this dispute as some, if not many, lawyers would rather escalate a dispute rather than resolve one as after all lawyers do not make their money and meet their billable hour targets by settling cases as soon as possible despite this being in the best interests of their clients.

If this stepped initial stage does not resolve the dispute or there are issues left to be discussed the traditional next tier would be the involvement of an independent third party, either to facilitate the negotiations in an informal process or in a Mediation where the parties, together with their legal teams would engage a third party to assist them in resolving the issue or dispute.

Next step, which is optional, is to involve an expert to determine a particular issue. This may be alongside another process (Mediation, Adjudication, Arbitration) and any decision can be binding or non-binding.

The traditional last tier would be for the parties to seek recourse to Adjudication or Arbitration where a decision is imposed by a third party. Of course, there is also the court; it is technically a method of Dispute Resolution but it is lengthy, expensive and definitely the last resort.

In order for these types of clauses to be effective it is of paramount importance that they are drafted carefully and appropriately but also that the interpretation of the clause is sufficiently clear in order to avoid confusion – whether that be genuine or tactical.

It would also be prudent to include a separate good faith provision that covers and binds the entire agreement including the escalating Dispute Resolution clause in order to prevent any party from submitting to a Dispute Resolution clause but with no real or genuine intention of adhering to the written word.

Conclusion:

Whilst it might appear to be an obvious statement but 'getting it right from the start' has to be the aspirational objective when contracts or agreements are being prepared and drafted. Too often are the agreements or contracts rushed through because of other, often commercial, pressures or 'we'll deal with the fine print later on' and it never gets done and this is not effective Dispute Avoidance, in reality it is dispute creation.

Trying to retrospectively alter terms or conditions after the 'ink has dried' is fraught with serious complications and it is therefore far more preferable to agree and sign up to a contract that is agreed and understood from the outset and is *'fit for purpose'*. This also has to apply to the 'boilerplate' provision as well as the Dispute Resolution clause because when issues arise, as they so often will, that is the first place parties and their legal teams will look and if it's been poorly drafted and is not appropriate for the context of the agreement itself then there cannot be any comfort or certainty for the parties in the avoidance of legal disputes.

Recognition of disputes, identifying conflict & Dispute Management systems

Disputes of any kind develop over a series of phases or steps. Professor Friedrich Glasl described this process in his book "Confronting Conflict" (1999), as an escalator.

The first phase he called 'Win-Win' was summarised as: tension; increasing unpleasant debate and preparation for adversarial action.

The second phase he called 'Win-Lose' was summarised as: poor communications; litigation or Arbitration; exaggerated claims and the exchange of threats.

The third and final phase he called 'Lose-Lose' was summarised as: destructive blows; aim to destroy the other party; will to win is all encompassing; the drive to defeat the other party is stronger than self-preservation.

What Professor Glasl illustrates, is that when communications break down, parties lose the ability to compromise and start the process of assessing their positions based on rights, rather than needs. Commercial relationships only work, when both parties see their needs being met and programmes are managed based on compromise, not strict legal rights. While contracts clearly have a legal foundation, over their lifetime they must be interpreted and reinterpreted countless times and agreement found on differences that arise. In most cases that is precisely what happens in most contracts, otherwise they would not be used in commerce. It is in those cases where these differences escalate into conflict and conflict into disputes because communication and the ability to compromise is lost, that Glasl's escalator takes over.

So, what can a business do to recognise disputes and identify the risk of them to avoid getting onto Glasl's escalator or once on it to get off, before it reaches the top?

Recognition that disputes will occur:

As with assessing any business process, there must first be a recognition that an event of risk will occur and that there should be an established procedure for dealing with it. A dispute in the context of running a business, while unidentifiable and whether internal or external, should be an anticipated event. A risk that every business can, through analysis, recognise it can then be planned for and assessed appropriately.

Increasingly businesses are preparing for disputes by instituting 'Dispute Management systems'. These are formal internal processes institutionalising how conflict, both internal and external to the business when it arises, will be dealt with. The objective being to implement a policy by which corporate risk can be dealt with in a systematic and rational manner. This avoids the haphazard and often emotional approach taken by most businesses to a dispute and permits the business to retain a certain amount of control over the process of the dispute and its ultimate outcome.

Steps in implementing a Dispute Management system:

Risk is the possibility that an event will occur and adversely affect the achievement of business objectives.

A risk factor is a circumstance (internal or external to the organisation), which tends to increase the likelihood of an adverse event occurring.

So how do you assess the risk of conflict to a business and then measure the risk factors to establish a Dispute Management system?

Stages of risk assessment:

a. Risk Identification: Identify characteristics and quantify conflict risks to the business
b. Risk Evaluation: Evaluate the potential significance of the risks indicating the relative importance of each risk factor to the business

Some common conflict risk factors to consider:

1. Review the contracts and programme management process – what are its weaknesses and where can it be improved when conflict arises?
2. Review supply chain terms and conditions, management and controls – are they robust enough and how is conflict dealt with when it arises?
3. Is there formal project management and conflict awareness training?

4. Is there a formal Dispute Resolution process that provides objective guidelines once a conflict is identified?
5. Does past programme and contract performance indicate poor governance and lack of management oversight?
6. Does the business suffer from weakness in financial controls?
7. Is there a lack of contract and programme monitoring and review?
8. Are there clear contract clauses dealing with conflict management and are they being implemented?
9. Is there a written contracts review procedure whereby business objectives and risk factors are identified and mitigation processes put in place?
10. Is there an adequate contracts management sign off procedure?
11. Is there a formal review of conflict history arising from poorly performed contracts and lessons learned reporting? What has been learned from past adverse events?
12. Is there a conflict review procedure, which formally reviews the status of all conflicts on a 3 or 6 month basis, with recommendations and a resolution road map?

Designing an effective Dispute Management system:

Once areas of conflict risk are identified, an effective Dispute Management system can be inserted into a formal Alternative Dispute Resolution ("ADR") policy, incorporating the following processes:

- A forensic review of traditional conflict points both internal and external to the business

- Drafting of model dispute clauses to adequately cover identified conflict risks
- Adequate training and education of employees dealing with customers, contractors and suppliers to the business
- Consideration of appropriate ADR tools to address conflict risks to the business and where appropriate building them into the dispute clause
- Systematic review of actual conflicts facing the business through a formal conflict review procedure to assess the most appropriate means for resolution utilising ADR tools.

Conclusion:

- Recognise that disputes will occur
- Disputes develop over a series of phases
- Move to a needs not wants based negotiation strategy
- Identify conflict risks in the business leading to disputes
- Implement a Disputes Management System to minimise disputes.

Assisted deal making

Negotiating a deal is something common to all businesses. It is the essence of what business people do all the time. However, it is not necessarily true that simply because you have experience negotiating that you will get the best result. There are many factors that go into a good deal and perhaps the most important is that there is balance between the position of both parties.

As we know parties set out to negotiate the best deal for themselves, often failing to recognise the position of the other party. In most cultures, such positional negotiation is natural, but it does not necessarily lead to the best result. It also allows for impasse to develop in the negotiation, as each party scrambles for their position to be accepted. Many negotiations fail because the parties have not or refuse to recognise the needs of their counterpart. Even where deals are made they are often assessed as a 'legal claim waiting to happen'. Such deals are of course of little value to either party. They invariably result in the minimum possible, other possibilities being undiscovered or ignored. How then can we make better deals, which recognise the needs and interests of the other party to the negotiation; one answer is the use of assisted deal making.

Assisted deal making utilises the assistance of a third-party neutral to help with the negotiation. This method of deal negotiation is sometimes also called deal Mediation. Assisted deal making has some of the attributes associated with Mediation, but is also different, given that there is of course no dispute. The techniques used by the deal Mediator will however often be similar. These will include:

- Helping the parties to move from positional to principled negotiation
- Clarifying issues and interests and in particular each party's needs
- Breaking down an obstacle, dealing with smaller issues one-by-one
- Reality checking positions
- Changing the balance of risk and reward sharing
- Helping to frame the deal structure and progress made
- Instigating working groups to deal with specific issues
- Taking strategic breaks and allowing cooling off periods
- Identifying potential solutions to break deadlock

Suitable areas for deal Mediation are:

1. Joint ventures
2. Franchise agreements
3. Intellectual Property ("IP") agreements
4. Commercial agreements
5. Mergers and acquisitions
6. Complex and multi-party matters

What does the neutral bring to the negotiation table that the parties themselves cannot achieve?

Each side to a commercial negotiation tends to manage risk by looking at the other party as an opponent. This attitude to negotiation leads to a certain distrust and views of opportunism on the part of the other side. What the deal Mediator brings to the table is addressing the issues from an objective and neutral position.

The deal Mediator helps by creating a realistic view of each side's position and intention. Many of the tools that the deal Mediator will utilise will be recognisable to the Mediation of a commercial dispute. Credibility and trust will of course be crucial assets that the deal Mediator has to possess, as in any Mediation.

So how does it work in practice:

What the deal Mediator can bring to a commercial negotiation is the imposition of structure and timetable, just as in a commercial dispute. Parties can be briefed beforehand on what is needed to be prepared for the negotiation and what will be expected from them. This will include a framework in which parties are encouraged to list their needs and objectives in a constructive proposal that benefits the overall deal and not simply their own side. Within this structure the Mediator will work to facilitate an agreement that is acceptable to both parties. The tool known to all Mediators of reality checking will help to bring the parties from positional to more interest based considerations. The deal Mediator will engage with the parties both jointly and separately to establish the relevant contribution and best outcome for a mutually agreeable deal. The deal Mediator will also be able to gauge the strengths and weaknesses of the participants and determine how best to utilise interpersonal relationships to get the best deal. This begins by helping the parties to create effective negotiating teams, to set an agenda and timetable for the negotiations and to assign a role for specialists that might have to be brought in to give opinions on aspects of the deal. This structural framework, put in place by the neutral, in discussion with the parties, is a key element to having an effective and successful negotiation.

The structure of the deal Mediation will involve more roundtable meetings with the parties, rather than caucusing (having private meetings). It will however at times, be necessary to have private meetings in order to fact check and bring reality to the negotiation table. The Mediator will act more like the chairperson of the meeting, tasking, directing and timetabling. There is value in the deal Mediator challenging the parties where it is felt that discussions are leading nowhere or getting stuck in unrealistic positions. The deal Mediator, more than a Mediator in a dispute, can make suggestions as to possible outcomes and be creative in suggesting deal structures. As a neutral, and seen as being objective, the parties are likely to be more receptive to such suggestions.

Conclusion:

This process of neutral assisted negotiation entails that one by one each side's concerns are reviewed and addressed. The key for the dealmaker is to find a balance which each side considers to be a fair apportionment of risk and reward. Through the deal Mediator, momentum can be created so that energy is directed towards a positive outcome, rather than being distrustful of the other party and their motives. Deal Mediation, perhaps even more than in mediating commercial disputes, can truly lead to a 'Win-Win' solution, whereby a more effective and balanced agreement can be achieved and these are much less likely to lead to future disputes. Deal Mediation, when used collaboratively and correctly, is effective Dispute Aviodance.

Boardroom issues & executive coaching

While boardrooms do exhibit disputes, conflict and tension they are frequently kept under the surface until a major crisis arises when they may go into overdrive and cause the organisation lasting damage.

Evaluators frequently comment on the fact that there is little challenge in a particular board – indeed, when reviewing the minutes it is sometimes written that *"It is as if the non-executive directors were not in the room!"*

This avoidance of conflict is not healthy for boards of directors, a fact recognised by the Guidance on Board Effectiveness, which stated that *"An effective board should not necessarily be a comfortable place. Challenge as well as teamwork is an essential feature."*[1] Yet despite this, boards still find conflict and tension difficult – as research has shown *"66% of top teams are too inhibited to raise uncomfortable issues and consequentially allow for a continued and slow deterioration of the organisation."*[2]

Conflict and tension can be positive:

So how should you, as a director, accept that conflict and tension are necessary components of a board wishing to avoid a dispute or at least resolve a dispute if it has arisen.

---

1. UK Guidance on Board Effectiveness, Financial Reporting Council, London.
2. Kakabadse and Kakabadse 2014 cited from The Company Secretary: Building Trust through Governance, ICSA and Henely Business School 2014.

First, it is important that the culture of the board is one in which challenge and tension - healthy tension that is – can be aired. In their *report on the culture of boards in 2016*[3] the Financial Reporting Council outlined the following factors as important to a positive board culture:

- Recognise the value of culture
- Demonstrate leadership
- Be open and accountable
- Embed and integrate
- Assess, measure and engage
- Align values and incentive
- Exercise stewardship

The really important one is being open and accountable. Many boards are not. Many evaluations of boards state that difficult issues are not tackled well in the boardroom and that there is a preponderance of passive aggressive behaviour with the latter only exhibiting a presence when matters are urgent and when it is perhaps too late to rectify a particular situation. And, of course, at this and any stage, aggression is of no benefit.

Dealing with board conflict:

So what are the best ways of dealing with conflict and tension with a view to avoiding full scale disputes?

3. Corporate Culture and the Roles of Boards, Financial Reporting Council, London, 2016.

- First, you should recognise that being on a board requires two key components: integrity and courage. It goes without saying that at this level you should have the first although again we have all seen examples of where this is not the case. The second is vital too: the board is indeed, at times, an uncomfortable place. You need to have the courage to disagree with others on the board, to take a minority and unpopular view, to be an outlier. This can be a challenge but you are on the board not to be popular, nor to cater to people's sensitivities, but to act in the best interests of the organisation and its various stakeholders: shareholders, employees and customers and the like. That may mean making a difficult choice.

- Second, the way in which the board is constructed, will determine to an extent whether conflict and tension can be used to deter dispute and factions. This is very much the role of an effective chair creating the right environment for challenge to thrive and drive the effective board and organisation. This is where the chair is akin to a skilled Mediator: first and foremost they need to be an effective facilitator. Peter Drucker had a mantra: *"Listen first, speak last"*[4]. This means that the chair needs to bring in all board members and ensure that they are able to have their say. More importantly, s/he must allow debate to be transparent and open without letting emotion get out of hand – a sometimes difficult balancing act. And finally, the Chair must not dominate and give their views first.

---

4. Peter Drucker, What makes an Effective Executive Harvard Business Review June 2004.

- Third, the board needs to develop the right culture. In his classic Harvard study *"What makes great boards great"*[5]. Jeffrey Sonnenfeld stated a number of characteristics of great boards. These included:

    o   Creating a climate of trust and candour
    o   Fostering a culture of open dissent
    o   Ensuring individual accountability

- Fourth, the listening Drucker advises is one that board members must also adopt. Disputes frequently arise because members of the board are not really listening to each other: this is not just a case of simple interruption but a determination of wanting to get their views across without assessing what others say. This leads to misunderstanding which then develops into factionalism and dispute amongst board members.

- Fifth, tension and conflict will only be managed where there is trust among the members of the board and they feel they can raise issues. There are indeed no stupid questions here and all directors should be able to feel they can ask any question however basic it might seem: a basic question may elicit an answer that resolves an issue quickly and painlessly rather than allowing it to develop into a full blown dispute. A trusting board, even a trusting team, will not have a fear of conflict and will be willing to raise any matter as well as to listen to the debate. Indeed, such boards tend to have a deeper level of debate and achieve solutions to challenges much more quickly than less effective boards.

5. Jeffrey Sonnenfeld, Harvard Business Review, Boston, 2002.

- Finally, as the ICSA and Henley Business School report on *Conflict and Tension in the boardroom*[6] identified there are a number of methods to manage conflict so that it does not get out of hand including:

  o Explicitly acknowledging concerns during board meetings
  o Face-to-face conversations
  o Depersonalising issues by remembering that the board has a higher purpose (separating people and problem)
  o Resolving matters such as personality clashes outside the boardroom on a more informal basis leaving more material matters such as strategy and decision issues for the board itself.

Courage and integrity:

So in your role as an effective board member you need to be able to embrace conflict and tension while ensuring that it does not turn into dispute and factionalism. Remembering the two mantras of courage and integrity should help you achieve this.

---

6. ICSA/Henley Business School 2017.

Executive Coaching:

Executive coaching - indeed coaching in general – has many attributes which helps avoid, manage and resolve disputes and disagreements.

At an initial stage, coaching allows you the opportunity to have someone guide you through the issues you may be facing within or around the boardroom. Having a coach – as an independent and confidential party – to be able to help you work through these types of issues can be invaluable. It needs to be borne in mind, however, that a coach is not there to 'advise' you or to resolve your issues - that is for you to do. However, a coach will guide you to think about the right way to resolve issues, to ask the right questions and to think about them in the context of resolution. This helps you see issues in an objective light, focusing on what you might do differently in the future – a different way to act or listen perhaps – with a view to ensuring disputes do not arise or are exacerbated.

Coaching:

Coaching, however, has a wider remit in helping avoiding, managing and resolving disputes. Two key attributes of coaching are contracting and listening. Contracting is being clear - really clear, precisely clear – about what the coach and the client will discuss. Contracting can take up much of a typical coaching session but without clear contracting at the beginning – what precisely is the issue – there can be no resolution. If you think how often disagreements begin and escalate because each side does not understand the other then you can appreciate why contracting can help in conflict. Being clear about the other side's position – putting yourself in their shoes – will often resolve an issue of its own or at least allow you to alter your position without losing face. The disagreement may well have arisen because there was a misunderstanding between the parties where a full appreciation of each other's views might have avoided any tension or conflict in the first place.

This leads to the other key skill in coaching which can be applied to resolving disputes. That is listening – real listening as Druker, mentioned above, means that a good manager should listen first and speak last, rather than jumping straight in with your views or talking over the other side. Allowing them to put their view across without interruption is another way to fully discuss and deep dive all relevant matters which in turn may go a long way to resolving or even preventing disputes and disagreements.

So coaching can be a valuable attribute in the boardroom both as a skill in itself and also if you need an independent party to coach you through some of the issues you are facing.

PART 2

Managing Disputes

Sometimes having the right skills and policies is just not enough and disputes arise that need to be managed effectively before they escalate into full-blown litigation.

Effective management of disputes includes accepting the need that negotiating intelligently with a focus on co-operation not confrontation is required by all. Couple this together with accurate risk assessment and preparing the best case rather than arguing the points you wish you had and the management of a dispute to an agreed outcome will be far more achievable and this is the most time efficient and cost effective way to manage a dispute and conclude its resolution.

Inefficient management of disputes will cause deeper divisions thereby making a resolution harder to achieve. It will also exacerbate risk, increase exposure to greater legal fees, increased insurance premiums and more and more time that could and should be devoted to other projects and opportunities will be required to be expended on the dispute. All of these are inherently bad for business and its future as commercial opportunities may be lost, employees may leave, relationships with current clients and customers may not be given the time needed to maintain and develop them and all at the same time legal fees are depleting the profitability of the business.

Co-operation -v- confrontation

We are in an age of fighting. Our culture is to fight for our rights, to seek justice through the courts, to oppose those who have different views but most passionately of all to win and to be proved right. Through the power of social media and the rapidity now that versions of events are disseminated across the world it has perhaps become even more important to be proved right or to put it more accurately that your version of the truth is accepted and that the courts, society, business colleagues, clients and customers, as well as friends and family, are aware that you were right. These habits are difficult to change.

Western culture, or more particularly, British and American culture, is founded on positional negotiation. That invariably means building the best possible position and giving little, slowly. This usually either leads to deadlock and a failed negotiation, or to one party getting the better of the other. Both results almost always damage the relationship. However, co-operating to achieve the best outcome for all parties is, for most people, counter cultural. There is this perceived belief in needing to be validated, to be vindicated and to be seen to be right.

So therefore setting aside the need to win, and working alongside others, can be quite a challenge. It involves a resistance to instinct and a stepping back from 'rights'. It means listening instead of demanding, exploring options instead of quarrelling, seeking interests rather than fighting claims. It needs extra effort, but the outcome, and the experience of negotiating in a better way, can be life changing.

Making the effort to co-operate is only the start, there are other challenges:

- We are all different
- Because of that we see the same facts and events differently
- Different nationalities view time, seniority and justice differently
- Power imbalance can be significant
- When trust is broken it is difficult to rebuild
- People don't necessarily play by the same rules
- Some people want to be told the answer
- Some people don't care about preserving relationships

We are all different:

We want to be respected and to retain our dignity. The need for food and shelter and warmth and human contact are basic to us all. But we are also unique, each one of us is different and so our emotions, our demeanour, our way of relating to others, of making decisions, our response to conflict all are unique and all affect the way we communicate and negotiate in our chosen careers and profession. Also, we all see the same facts and events differently, for a whole lot of reasons – it could be due to our education, gender, age, ethnicity and a whole lot more. It does not necessarily mean our interpretation, our 'truth', is more right or wrong, it is just different.

Add to all of that the cultural dimension, and we are in a minefield that could inhibit effective co-operation.

Cultural differences:

The first question is what do we mean by culture? The best answer to that question is 'it is the way we do it here'. It is so easy to assume that culture means ethnicity, custom, religion, tradition and so on. That may well be so but it is so much more complex than that. Every business has its own culture and, unless you come from that business there is a danger of being unaware of particular sensitivities that may have an impact on any communication or negotiation. Indeed, even being a member of that business is no guarantee of knowing all the sensitivities. We are all individuals with our own characteristics, and few of us conform to the assumed group characteristics. We may well conform in many ways to a group identity but no human being acts all the time in an individually predictable way. So the danger of such ignorance is that we make assumptions, usually based upon stereotypes, and assumptions are a weakness.

Changing assumptions into fact:

Any position based upon assumptions is a weak position. It should always be questioned and ways determined that can change assumptions into facts. The fewer assumptions there are, the less risk and therefore the stronger the position taken. Researching, finding other's experience of the individual or group, even enquiring of the individual or group itself, will provide more information and therefore build more confidence before entering into the communication or negotiation itself. So be open to learning that 'they' are not as expected. The rule must be to turn assumptions into facts. It will lead to a far stronger, and therefore less risky, position.

Time, seniority, decision-making:

Having said all that, there are some important cultural issues that need to be clarified before business can commence. Time is one of them. Most western cultures view time as critical and are used to deadlines and the need to close so that the next issue can be addressed. Some cultures see time as endless and have a need to consider, discuss and gestate before any decision can be reached. This can be very frustrating to a deadline-controlled negotiator, but prior knowledge will allow the negotiator to plan a strategy that will use the time efficiently.

Similarly, the matter of authority could be an issue. In some cultures the most senior person tends to be the one who speaks the least. Indeed, the real decision-maker may not even be present. In others, the final decision may need to be collective, so taken back to the group by its representatives before a solution can be ratified. This underlines the importance of clarifying the situation beforehand. Who is the decision-maker? Does a deal have to be ratified? What time-scale is involved?

Fairness or justice (or both):

People come to the negotiation table with their own belief as to what is fair. Each will have their own set of values and their own need to leave the negotiation with dignity. That underlines the importance of getting the headline agreed (what is the desired outcome) and establishing each party's needs (rather than wants). The first will provide the common focus and goal and the second will shape the eventual deal.

Power imbalance:

Parties in a negotiation are rarely of equal power. What equalises power is preparation. Understanding the other side's needs, understanding your own and, most importantly, understanding when to walk away from the negotiation. Better deals, or no deal, may be found in a different way.

Broken trust:

Trust is key to effective outcomes in negotiation. Parties need to believe that both sides are negotiating in good faith and that they will stick to the deal when it is agreed. When trust is broken, as often happens in disputes, it is very difficult (even near impossible) to restore. It takes time and outward demonstrations of good faith. Much better to reinforce trust rather than to break it.

Different rules:

Some people cannot accept that better deals arise from co-operation. This can lead to a discordant negotiation, where one party wants to co-operate and the other wants to win. Where one sees this as a joint problem needing a joint solution and the other doesn't care. In such circumstances it takes courage to hold on to being co-operative, especially when the other side appears to be bullying. But being co-operative is the best option and worth holding on to.

In some cases the negotiator does not have the authority to seal the deal or is unwilling to take the responsibility. This should be disclosed at the beginning and a strategy agreed as to how that authority may be obtained once a deal is done.

Relationships:

In the long term 'beating' the other side may not be a satisfactory outcome. A good working relationship is one that can cope with differences. Indeed a healthy organisation will value those differences and work on how they can be used to benefit the organisation.

A good working relationship tends to make it easier to get a good substantive outcome (for both sides) and good substantive outcomes tend to make good relationships even better.

Conclusion:

Positional (adversarial) bargaining results in the minimum deal that gets agreement but resentment and bitterness is likely to remain.

Co-operative negotiation, seeing the situation as an exercise in joint benefit, softens the edges of negotiation and allows outcomes that benefit all parties. The parties are able to seek solutions that enrich a deal rather than pare it to the absolute minimum. A co-operative negotiation will also provide an outcome that is far more likely to last and it might even open the door to other commercial opportunities for further mutual benefit.

Third party intervention

We have already set out how a third party can help in getting parties to agree a deal. Third parties can also play a crucial role in negotiating intelligently within the space of managing disputes. In this context, when we negotiate we are trying to obtain or bring about by discussion a positive change in a dispute or perhaps find a way over or through an obstacle or difficult route. To do that intelligently means that we do so in a knowledgeable and insightful way. This suggests a far from haphazard process; careful planning and choices are normally involved. This is the same when it comes to using third parties. Often our thoughts jump ahead to the use of Mediators or Arbitrators as the obvious third party in a dispute process. However, whilst valid, these options are more back-ended to the process and they are not the only options open to parties in a conflict or escalating situation. We will consider what roles third parties can play in managing disputes, who they might be and whether or not they need to be independent or impartial.

We do not need to be bound by preconceived convention when working out how to negotiate; the help we need can come from different places. Ultimately, the objective in a given situation should be the singular goal of getting to the other side of the dispute. Of course, there will be more than one party to a dispute, yet ultimately resolving the dispute is important to each party and whilst understanding the other's situation, as all good negotiation books and strategies will insist, each party needs to consider what process is best for themselves. A third party can be any person or even an institution that gets involved in managing a dispute. They may be directly or indirectly connected to the dispute or independent from it. Third parties may be asked to the table or sometimes they offer their help and when accepted they too are invited. Third parties may support one side in the negotiation or operate across the divide working with all the parties involved. At other times however, a third party intervention may be imposed which alters the level of choice suggested here, a topic on which we shall touch later. Outside of an imposed third party, any invited third party can bring relief to one or more of the parties, particularly in helping a party to reality-test their position, prepare the case and work healthily with their emotions. To understand this in practice we will consider a couple of settings and in each we will make the assumption that the parties involved in a dispute have not formalised the dispute towards a resolution scenario such as court or Mediation; those will be regarded in the coming sections.

Learning from commercial and workplace situations:

Consider the position of just one party in a commercial contract. They have a wealth of third parties available to them that are both internal and external to their organisation. It is obvious that an external legal advisor can play a role in assisting a party to manage a contractual negotiation, yet a likely question of 'is someone from inside their own organisation a third party?' is worthy of consideration. Managers are often called upon to intervene in situations of internal workplace conflict and they normally are asked to review situations outside of their regular domain, thus effectively acting as a third party. They can play multiple roles such as an inquirer or a Mediator, but they are not always well prepared or successful. If they are ill-equipped or poorly trained the outcomes in the workplace may not be as desired or even fair.[1] It is clear that internal people can and do play a role as a third party however, in consideration of the success needed, defining the role that internal third parties play is as essential as it would be for an external third party.

We should note that there are often established internal boundaries and policies within a company which mandate negotiation teams to call on specific internal third parties, for example those who set price levels or commercial limits of liabilities. These are assumed as a norm. However, sometimes a fresh pair of eyes in a situation can truly help find breakthroughs. Using someone else's creative skills, bouncing off ideas with another or allowing one's own position to be challenged by a colleague are all valuable concepts that can be deployed in negotiation. The same can be said of external third parties and it is important to note that lawyers are not the only option. It might be just as valid in a given situation to employ other experts to help. Expert witnesses have been used effectively for years, but often in a court or Arbitration setting, sadly after a litigation has already taken its financial toll. If we reimagine the concept of what an expert witness can be it helps us consider other resources that might assist to make the negotiation intelligent. A retired commercial manager can help reflect strategies; a Mediator may act out of role to help explain future processes that motivate a party to negotiate sooner rather than commit more money to litigation a tax consultant might suggest alternatives that clears the way for a breakthrough in commercial negotiations.

In each method, the lead negotiator should be the one who manages

---

1. Karambayya R. and Brett J.M. (1989) Managers Handling Disputes: Third-Party Roles and Perceptions of Fairness. The Academy of Management Journal. 32 (4). pp. 687-704.

the process, even if someone offers their expertise or help it should be used intelligently. When it comes to using a third party across party boundaries we move more to the concept of facilitation, which will be addressed further in this Guide.

Learning from family situations:

One must acknowledge the positive and healthy role of third parties in managing family situations and in doing so it can trigger ideas for use across different sectors. For example, there are many voluntary arrangements involving third parties made by families to help themselves. This spans a spectrum from safe-space learning opportunities such as parenting courses; grievance counselling or marriage guidance through to the tougher end of intervention when things seem to be going bad.

In family situations a very evident symptom is often emotion linked to poor communication and behaviour. Emotions are in fact evident within every dispute because they involve people. In family conflicts the emotions are often very raw and a lot of third party work challenges participants such as parents to understand their own emotions before tacking the perceived issue. Hence, third parties who understand emotional intelligence or non-violent communication are extremely helpful in the case of families.[2] Not only here however, but a person with these skills can also help in a workplace, with a contract dispute or a community conflict and

2. See Rosenberg M. B. (2015) Nonviolent Communication - A Language of Life. Encinitas. PuddleDance Press. And Goleman D. (1996) Emotional Intelligence: Why it Can Matter More Than IQ. London. Bloomsbury.

these skills are regularly deployed by Mediators or counsellors in such circumstances.

The clear role of the third party is not to take away emotion in negotiation. If emotion is suppressed then it will remain and could erupt at the wrong time and in the wrong way. Understanding what is going on for one party emotionally in themselves is often a key to finding a way through the situation. Sometimes we have to admit we are so contained within the situation we find it hard to 'see the wood for the trees'; we get stuck and a skilled practitioner can help. Finding third party help in this area can really benefit negotiations early on.

In these contexts above, it is likely that those needing help will request it or help will be offered to them; they are always in control of the process and without labouring the point too much, they should be managing this intelligently. There is however a situation where third parties play a more imposed role. Take for example the real situation in which a mutual fund management company owned a minority stake in two listed companies who were heading for court. So, whilst this minority shareholder could not impose their will on the companies, as a serious stakeholder in this case they became aware of the situation and intervened with the global Chief Executive Officer ("CEO") of the two companies in question to avoid possible press and reputation issues, let alone think of financial implications – this was some four levels above the negotiation teams in question. Subsequently a representative of the CEO of one of the companies involved was instructed to fly to the regional office and then meet the other side. Negotiations concluded quickly with no subsequent recourse.

Conclusion:

A lead negotiator might consider consulting a specific number of internal and external third parties to create a knowledge bank of ideas and concepts for their plan. Do not just assume a lawyer is the answer in this situation (as it rarely is) consider alternative consultants, colleagues, friends and even family members to build a truly intelligent plan. At the negotiating stage independence or impartiality of third parties is less important; primarily they will be working for one of the parties. This does not preclude impartial third parties; however, using such people will be more in the realm of a Mediation itself.

Assessing risk

When all is said and done even if a Dispute Management system is in place or at least businesses have identified an 'escalator' it is imperative that businesses understand and have fully analysed their commercial risk in relation to the 'escalator' or dispute.

Without assessing the risk to the business of the dispute achieving an early resolution will be problematic and perhaps even impossible.

This applies to both sides of 'the fence' of a dispute; whether you are claiming or defending or the paying or receiving party. Right and wrong rarely comes into our thinking as most will persuade themselves that their version of events is the only thing that matters or perhaps even more cynically the lawyers have persuaded their clients that their case is worth pursuing or worth defending through the courts. However a blinkered approach can, and often does, merely lead to an escalation of the dispute without first undertaking any risk assessment of the costs, time, lost opportunities and fractured relationships that are inevitably part of a legally determined, right and wrong, dictated decision.

In assessing risk sensibly consideration has to be taken as to seeking a resolution as soon as practicable in order to try and achieve the 'Win-Win' situation. It is often commented that parties to a dispute will remark at some point, albeit often towards the end of the trial of the matter, that *'they never wanted this'* or more commonly *'they wish they'd never started this'*. It is actually more than likely that on more than one occasion during the protracted legal process that both parties will privately reflect and lament on the time wasted and money thrown away to lawyers and the legal system but once started it is naive of any litigating party to assume they can just walk away and cease the proceedings without adverse and onerous consequences.

Therefore parties in dispute need to be advised, counselled and at times told by their legal advisors that when it's all over it's only the parties that have to live with the outcome and the lawyers whilst they might talk about being 'on your side' they will move on to their next case and next client with little reflection whereas the parties have to move forward with the terms of the outcome on their shoulders and in their minds.

Every dispute carries within it an element of risk. Even a simple and straightforward 'unpaid invoice' dispute carries multiple layers of risk such as 'does the debtor have the money to pay' whereas the complex high-value multi-issue matters will inevitably possess a variety of significant risks to each party.

In assessing risk sensibly parties have to remain intrinsically involved in the decision-making process because they are the only ones who can decide if the risk of escalation is worth taking.

Control of the outcome needs to be vested in the stakeholders to the dispute for as long as possible, if this can be achieved with the aid and advice of lawyers then so much the better as the longer the parties to a dispute remain engaged, even if this includes positional and aggressive communication, the higher the possibility there is of the parties agreeing terms of settlement when legal costs, management time and commercial risk are reduced. By the time legal proceedings are issued the actual parties have lost overall control of the dispute as litigation, by its very nature, requires the devolution of control away from the parties to solicitors, barristers, cost advocates, insurers, experts and ultimately the court.

Litigation risk:

'There is no risk as we are going to win'. This is an all too common statement in litigation often emanating from a party in a positional attempt to convince themselves and their adversary they are indeed going to win.

In litigation there will always be a winner and a loser – 'the Win-Lose scenario' that is the basis of the adversarial court system – one side will be awarded judgment in their favour and the other will have judgment against them.

There is an assumption that the winner's costs are paid by the loser but that is not always the case. Even if a cost award is granted the 'winner' will never recover all of their legal expenditure despite what might be inferred, at best 75% of costs are generally recoverable but there are instances where the 'winning' side are not awarded payment of any of their legal costs whereas the traditional award to a 'winning' party is in the region of 60-75% of their legal costs. Therefore based on a simple win or lose litigation situation even 'winning' means there will be an element of loss. In addition, insurance premiums are no longer recoverable and must be paid from any settlement figure so in categorising litigation it might be more of a 'Lose-Lose' scenario.

Litigation is beset with uncertainty and risk in every stage of the process from the very first exchanges all the way through to a final trial and therefore managing these risks is as much of an important consideration as the facts or law relevant to the matter. There is no such thing as a 'guaranteed win' in litigation which is where the legal advisors bring into play the disheartening phrase of 'litigation risk'.

Litigation risk is broadly explained as the unknown factors in litigation such as 'a bad day in court', 'unexpected curve balls', 'a differing judicial interpretation' or simply 'error'; not that the latter will be openly admitted. Litigation risk is generally but quite arbitrarily estimated at between 20-25% in all cases and this is perceived to factor in the 'unknowns' inherent in every action. Accordingly even the most confident of statements of *'we are going to win'* has to be tempered to a maximum of 80% certainty of winning.

Litigation risk is rarely explained to clients at the very outset of the lawyers instruction and it is often relied on too heavily as the final trial approaches. Perhaps if litigation risk was fully set out, along with the costs of pursuing any action through to a final trial it would in itself act as its own Dispute Management system.

In reality litigation risk can only ever be assessed on a case-by-case basis and most lawyers will have tales to tell of a *'dead cert'* going *'pear shaped'* due to factors outside of their control (note it is always out of 'their' control). With any type of litigation there is risk and therefore it contains an element of a being a 'gamble' and the bigger the case naturally the level of risk increases and therefore so does the stakes. Always remember it is you and your business that takes the risk and accepts the gamble. If horse-racing was historically claimed to be the 'sport of kings' in that to win a small fortune you needed to invest a large one it is probably more pertinent that in actual fact the 'sport of kings' is now litigation in that to win a small fortune in court you need to spend a large one.

Inherently therefore there exists a significant proportion of risk that has to be assessed sensibly in all litigious disputes and failing to recognise it and to deal with it effectively could have severe consequences for the ill-prepared client.

The danger that flows from an initial failure to consider and effectively analyse risk and the merits (both in fact and law) of a dispute is that initial confidence can be eroded by the reactions of the other side. Accurately predicting replies from the other side happens rarely as most legalistic letters are not entirely focused on Dispute Avoidance, Management or Resolution but are instead crafted in such a fashion that best portrays a particular view or interpretation which in turn causes the almost certain response from the other side that entirely rejects and refutes the basis of the arguments. And so begins the interminable exchange of letters between lawyers that ratchets up the bellicoseness on each occasion as the warring parties try to 'win' the case in correspondence with the only real outcome being that costs rise dramatically.

This all too typical 'back-n-forth' of litigious correspondence rarely has any positive impact on the matter and its settlement. More often than not, especially in the paying client's eyes, this only corrodes the initial confidence artificially buoyed by the aggressive early barrage of words.

So even before litigation proceedings have been issued at court the initial belief of *'we are right'* may lessen to *'we may be right'* or *'we have a chance of winning'* and if there is a failure to have effectively analysed risk this could lead to the situation where 'battle lines' are drawn on an issue or dispute that actually needs to be urgently resolved not litigated over.

If matters have progressed, or perhaps more pertinently, if matters have deteriorated, litigation risk is an essential tool in the decision-making process of managing disputes. In assessing litigation risk sensibly a formal opinion on the merits of an action can be prepared by a party's legal team and ATE ("After The Event") insurance cover may be sought thereafter. This would enable the decision-making parties to make more rational and commercial choices in how they wish to proceed provided that an effective Dispute Management system is in place and crucially that the parties themselves remain in overall control.

The actual reality of assessing litigation risk is that a legal opinion or insurance cover will dramatically reduce the absolute certainty that a successful outcome will be achieved given the 20% of litigation risk added to the usual temperance of legal teams to overstate the clients' chances of success. Again the definition of 'success' needs to be carefully thought through as 'success' for the client might well look entirely different from how a legal team might define 'success'.

Moreover if a party has devolved decision-making responsibility and control of the dispute to legal advisors they have to realise that those third party advisors will have their own, in some cases separate, drivers and objectives in respect of an action and what may be a favourable outcome or defined as a 'success'.

Assessing the time and cost of conducting litigation is perhaps as crucial an element as establishing the merits of a claim or defence - after all there is little tangible benefit in spending more in legal costs and lost management time than the claim or defence is actually worth. Therefore assessing risk sensibly in litigation terms is not just about winning or losing but it is also about what is it going to cost the party, in terms of time, money and reputation, to get to court.

If litigation is pursued without having first assessed the risk and having established the commercial consequences of what effect a claim or a defence or the overall result may have on a business, including any reputational impact, this is evidently not a sensible way to proceed. Furthermore consideration has to be given to the costs and time involved in allowing an issue to escalate and fester into a dispute and a legal action.

It is also worth noting that detailed assessment of risk should not just occur at the outset of litigation or a dispute but also throughout the resolution or litigation process.

Disputes will often become so deeply engrained into a business or individual's psyche that before long the assessing risk sensibly approach has been replaced with the dreaded phrase *'it's a matter of principle'*.

While principles are to be admired generally they should be feared when litigating. The insolvency and bankruptcy courts are overwhelmed with businesses or individuals respectively who have litigated over principles; and at the end no party wants to be left with nothing but an empty pocket and the all too familiar story that begins with *'if I could wind the clock back I'd never have started this in the first place'* and remember that the legal teams won't be stood facing those same perils.

Insurance policies are often also quoted as a safety net for potential litigants and whilst they might offer some respite over base legal costs there is a need to fully analyse the details of the policies over payment of VAT on fees, whether disbursements are included and what types of cases are actually insured for in the first place. Having an active insurance policy is part of assessing risk sensibly but reliance on it also needs careful consideration especially when assessing time frames (as insurance led legal actions also tend to take longer to conclude due to the sheer volume of caseload of the insurer appointed panel lawyers) and what costs are including and not included and finally the consequences of activating the insurance policy itself. It might therefore not be a pragmatic application of assessing risk sensibly to blindly pass the matter to insurers and their appointed solicitors as such a course of action can only cede control of the matter further away from you and also even increase you to other financial and commercial disputes not envisaged or predicted at the time of the 'escalator' event.

Conclusion:

It must make sense when a dispute occurs, to review the possible outcomes and assess the risk of each. It is far better to be realistic early on and so avoid the cost (personal and business), and wasted time in pursuing a case on a principle or emotional grounds. The earlier this is done, the sooner a strategy can be devised to achieve a cost-effective outcome. Commercial pragmatism is however not usually the first response when a business becomes embroiled in a dispute; the reaction tends to be a little more 'colourful'.

However if there is a procedure for the effective assessment of risk or a Dispute Management system is in place it will greatly assist the business to evaluate the situation far more astutely and appropriately and perhaps most critically of all it will enable the business to be in control of their outcome and therefore any terms of settlement.

At the very base level when all is said and done the first thing the business needs to carefully consider is whether the *juice is worth the squeeze*.

Preparing the best case

It has been discussed above that in order to effectively manage disputes this requires intelligent negotiation which in part involves a balance of co-operation and confrontation as well as the use of third party intervention. However there is a third strand to negotiating intelligently in managing disputes and that is 'making the best arguments'.

This might well appear to be an obvious comment insofar as it is neither pragmatic nor beneficial to propound inferior, ill-conceived or erroneous opinions in the expectation that favourable terms of settlement will be agreed on the back of such. Making the best arguments is a far wider concept than merely 'leading with your best point' and hoping it will be accepted and not rebuffed by the receiving party.

Making the best arguments and how and by whom they are delivered is a vital component to any intelligent negotiation.

In order for the best arguments to be presented they need to be fully detailed and 'stress tested' to ensure that the terms or basis of the argument do not unravel when it is challenged or analysed by the other side. After all it would be uncommon, but it is accepted that it is plausible, that one party's 'best argument' is not countered and accepted without any debate at all.

Therefore part of effective and efficient Dispute Management and intelligent negotiation is to be well prepared. In part this preparation lies in the hands of any advice being given by third parties but responsibility for the preparatory work should not be devolved entirely. After all, disputes are personal (whether they involve businesses or individuals) and therefore ultimately settlements are personal.

If matters have progressed to requiring third party involvement (for example lawyers) battle lines are likely to have been mapped out, formal letters sent and received where positions and arguments will have been set out and probably, as mentioned above, not accepted by the other.

The exchange of correspondence is part of preparing the case and assisting in the making of the best arguments - sometimes and depending on the advice and whether lawyers are involved there is a tendency to be overly belligerent and positional adopting the approach of *'getting your retaliation in first'* however as set out above this strategy is only a short term option and rarely beneficial and one that is utterly incongruent to the principles of Dispute Management and intelligent negotiation.

This is not presenting a persuasive case or even the best argument but an argumentative one and the natural reaction to it is to argue or fight back thereby further polarising positions and reinforcing the move towards hostility and mistrust which are factors that will be ruinous to any negotiation process. It also means that the lawyers acquire ever more control over the dispute itself and with each letter sent and exchanged the actual parties are taken further and further away from Dispute Management.

Lawyers should instinctively protect their clients and in the main they do so by presenting a legally robust and insistent standpoint. The response is usually to meet 'fire with fire', aggression with more aggression and so on until the salient even meritorious 'best arguments' of one side's case are lost 'in the heat of battle'. This approach, which might be perfectly correct in some situations, is far from ideal and unlikely to persuade a party that the other side has an argument or a point worth considering let alone accepting.

In order for arguments to be acknowledged they need to have merit and substance. For example one illustration is a pre-action counterclaim for un-particularised consequential losses that conveniently outweighs the claim value; this is often taken as just a 'try on' and fails to have the effect that such an argument was intended to have. In a heated and long standing dispute it is often the 'kitchen sink' approach to assert as many lines of attack or defence as possible in the belief that at least one will be effective; this is best evidenced when parties to a dispute list out their claims or defences. It is not envisaged that there will be total success on each and every item as it merely evidences the traditional positional negotiating tactic of demand a lot and give away little.

Therefore a persuasive case or best argument is to advance claims or defences that are sustainable in fact, law and, perhaps more pertinently for the purposes of negotiation, equity. For example a claim for a sum of monies that is genuine, thought through, stress-tested and well-presented is much more likely to succeed than a blanket demand for 'the kitchen sink'.

In preparing the best case careful consideration needs to be applied to the desired outcome as it would be unintelligent to assume that your best argument will automatically succeed. As above the usual practice, but not necessarily the best one, is to participate in 'horse-trading' or 'salami-slicing'. However as this is the typical approach it is often misleading as it is expected by the receiving party who tend to reciprocate with positional arguments of their own; this tends to actually prevent effective negotiation.

Advancing positions that are accurate, sustainable and not inflated for the purposes of archetypal negotiations actually forms the very core of presenting a persuasive case and making the best arguments.

Assuming that the best arguments have been prepared in a persuasive manner as commented upon above it is important to further consider the effect such will have on the receiving party; i.e. how will this be received. There are countless reactions and many are standard such as incredulity, anger, confusion and panic and of course any reaction might well be 'part of the negotiation game' but placing yourself in the shoes of the other party is a vital component of effective stress-testing and making the best arguments. After all advancing sustainable points and negotiating intelligently but not asking the question 'what effect will this have' or 'how will this be received' could nullify the best argument.

Conclusion:

Preparing the best case is so much more than leading with the strongest point. It has to be persuasive, stress-tested and presented appropriately. This applies both ways in a negotiation, whether you are claiming or defending and such an approach is far more likely to encourage and facilitate a coming together or a closing of the gap thereby leading to the effective management and resolution of the dispute.

The cynics may attempt to propound that this approach only works if all parties adopt the same approach but by making the best argument and through intelligent negotiation the other side's belligerence will be starved of the oxygen it needs to continue; in the end persuasion will out-last aggression.

Preparing the best case will manage disputes effectively and will protect a continuing business or personal relationship and will allow the parties a shared future without the resentment and bitterness that is left after a litigious battle.

Workplace Mediation

Workplace Mediation differs in its approach to that followed in commercial cases, where the Mediator's effort is often focused on facilitating the parties to a settlement before they go their separate ways. Workplace Mediation focuses on helping the parties start the process of rebuilding their relationships, most typically from a starting position of zero trust between them, with a view to them continuing to work together after the Mediation intervention.

In some circumstances the Mediation may focus on helping the parties re-establish a degree of trust or agree a set of rules where trust cannot be re-established, to enable them to agree a more limited goal, e.g. working together simply to achieve an agreed exit for one party at a future date or working together to prepare the business for sale.

Workplace Mediation involves the Mediator initially interviewing each party individually for between 1 to 1.5 hours, to get their side of the story, plus interviewing their line manager or the Human Resources lead. This is then followed typically by a one day session with the parties to: deal with the issues between them; achieve a commitment to continue working together and agree a simple action plan. In many cases therefore a breakthrough can be achieved in 1.5 days which enables the parties to continue working together.

Unlike in commercial cases there is little point in the Mediator pre-reading vast quantities of documents about who said what and when – the Mediator will identify the main issues to be addressed in the Mediation from the interviews.

Mediators apply a range of techniques, with some favouring Facilitative Mediation, where the Mediator leaves the decision-making to the parties, based on the premise that the parties have the best understanding of what they need for themselves and from each other, through to Transformative Mediation, where the Mediator works to foster and develop recognition between the parties, and aims to empower the parties to make their own decisions and take their own actions. This Transformative approach can be as robust as that deployed by Mediators in commercial Mediation.

What results can be achieved in a 1.5 day Mediation?

Case studies involving Individual parties:

1. Two Directors of a National Health Service ("NHS") Clinical Commissioning Group sat in adjoining offices and attended the same leadership team meetings but were not speaking to each other. Their relationship had deteriorated to the point where they were only emailing each other and as they had quickly moved into deeply entrenched positions the emails had progressed to being in capital letters and then colour coded. One party was in a hyper-emotional state and was on the brink of going off sick with stress. The Human Resources Director ("HRD") recognised at a relatively early stage that an intervention was required, at the point where a grievance was about to be raised about bullying and asked both parties to agree to a Mediation. The result of the Mediation was that both parties recognised how their relationship had deteriorated, and how distrust had developed around newly introduced project status reporting. They were able to agree to an action plan and to share it with

the HRD, and they were able to continue working. As a result of this Mediation no grievances were raised, and no sickness absence occurred. Similar cases which have not been mediated have taken up to two years to resolve in the NHS.

2. Two Directors of a company in London had reached the point where they could only sit in a room together if a witness was present. They were the only two Directors in the company, they had no Shareholder Agreement, and neither had available funds to buy the other party out. One Director had a highly emotional response and was totally unwilling to compromise. The Mediator had to accept the reality of their situation – you cannot wish or force the parties to compromise. After 1.5 days the parties were no further forward and the Mediator asked them to pause the process over Christmas and new year. They met again in late January and were able to agree a simple action plan to work together, including processes to include the senior management team when the two Directors were not in agreement. After a further two months one Director regained his confidence to the degree he felt empowered to assert his position about a longer term settlement, and at this point both parties then involved lawyers to enable that Director to be bought out. The impact of this Mediation was that both parties avoided significant legal costs being incurred during their 'totally irrational' phase and until the point where both parties were willing to do a business deal to buy one party out. The other benefit for the company was that five of the six members of the senior management team were willing to remain with the company during this time, when several had threatened to jump ship before the Mediation.

3. Three parties, all employees of a healthcare organisation in the private sector, providing safeguarding services. The trigger for the dispute had occurred 18 months earlier, when one employee raised a concern about how a Safeguarding Supervisor had recorded a case on the case management system, and then escalated the issue to a manager, who in turn escalated the issue further, resulting in a full investigation being conducted. After the 15 month investigation, it was concluded that the Safeguarding Supervisor had not done anything wrong and a simple clarifying discussion on day 1 could have managed the issue and prevented it escalating. At this 15 month point the Safeguarding Supervisor said she could no longer work with the other two colleagues. A Workplace Mediation took place at 18 months. After separating individual interviews the Mediator in effect conducted two parallel Mediations for the aggrieved employee and each colleague separately, due to the aggrieved employee's fear of being bullied in a joint meeting. Towards the end of the day all three parties came together and the aggrieved employee received an apology from each colleague. The power of the apology! The three parties reached an agreement to work together again. The impact of this Mediation was that the organisation retained three highly skilled and hard to recruit clinical resources.

Case study involving teams:

1. Solicitors' Partnership. The Mediator was brought in at the point where a regional firm of solicitors was on the point of partnership dissolution due to issues in the leadership team. The presenting issue was described as being the impact on the harmonious

running of the partnership of one 'problem partner' who was being disruptive to the extent that several of the partners wanted him out. The Mediator interviewed all the partners by phone and produced a report for the leadership team distilling the issues to be addressed. The Mediator then facilitated two meetings of the leadership team, using a mix of Mediation techniques. The breakthrough point came when the other partners realised that the problem partner's disruptive actions were all due to his frustration about him having a clear vision for the business, and his desire for the adoption of more rigorous business processes to drive profitability. In a totally unexpected outcome, the resolution was for the 'problem partner' to become the next CEO. An action plan was agreed which included the incumbent CEO stepping down within a short period of time, and the problem partner being appointed as CEO.

Project Mentoring

Project Mentoring (sometimes called Project Mediation) involves the introduction of a Mediator, or a panel of Mediators, to a project at the onset. The purpose is to:

- Get buy-in to collaborative working
- Identify and polish communication skills
- Facilitate difficult conversations/meetings
- Identify at the earliest stage any weaknesses or 'pinch-points'
- Resolve conflict before it escalates
- Monitor effectiveness

This is not Deal Mediation, although the Mediator may be involved in the contract negotiations. The Project Mentor's role is to iron out the 'rough edges' of relationships, documents and systems so that the project runs smoothly and achieves the common aim of finishing on time and within budget. That means a willingness to co-operate, realism in targets and expectations and a large dose of common sense.

Getting buy-in:

The UK government have adopted ISO 44001 Collaborative Business Relationship Management and it is now a significant part of the tender appraisal process. So in theory collaboration is the watchword and it applies to private and public organisations of all sizes so it is expected that this policy will become general industry practice. This is a great step away from competitive, protective working to working towards achieving a common aim and outcome. Project Mentoring only works if everyone involved sees its benefits and buys into its approach. It can be counter-cultural, especially in situations where a blame culture prevails. But it can be very rewarding.

Communication skills:

Poor communication is almost always the reason for conflict arising. Project Mentoring often involves training people who are involved in the project, not just in the systems and the project conditions but also in dealing with issues when they arise. This could be in questioning and listening skills, in raising self-awareness, in dealing with emotion and or moving from written communication to face-to-face. Some training may need to be bespoke for the group, or individual. All with the purpose of enabling a diverse group of people, with different personalities, skills and preferences, to work together in harmony.

The best outcome is for matters of conflict to be dealt with quickly and at the point of issue. In other words, by the people involved at the time. If this doesn't resolve the issue then the involvement of more senior people would be the next step, and only then, if that doesn't resolve the issue, the introduction of the Mentor. If the initial training has been effective then the Mentor will only be involved in the most difficult issues.

Facilitation:

One key benefit of the Project Mentor is being accepted as an independent who can chair meetings and who can be a neutral third party to facilitate difficult conversations. Often people are better able to talk through a third party as they find it difficult to speak one-to-one and the Mentor can manage the meeting or conversation in a way that keeps people focussed, keeps emotion positive and avoids losing face.

Identifying weak points:

There are two key methods of identifying weak points (people or process) that could lead to difficulties:

- Historic conflict – what has gone wrong in the past? What can we learn from it so that it is not repeated on this project? Where were the difficult relationships? How do we compensate for them?
- Regular feedback. Project Mentoring should involve a regular feedback system. It should have a facility for anonymous feedback so that people are not restrained in flagging up problems at an early stage, especially when relationships are challenged.

The Mentor will review the feedback and follow up any issues that have been identified, even anticipating issues before they arise or become serious. This is a key role as it provides an independent view of the project, both as an overview and also in detail. So problems can be dealt with early before they escalate into conflict.

Resolving conflict:

But despite all the preparation, training and monitoring, some issues can escalate into conflict and the Mentor's Mediation skills then become necessary. The Mentor is a known and trusted neutral and so should be in a position to help people resolve issues quickly and in a way that preserves relationships. It may be by use of a formal process, or informal facilitation. It may be at a neutral venue or 'on site'. The important thing is that the project is unaffected and that everyone's focus is on a quality product completed on time and in budget.

Choosing the Mentor:

Most schemes have an individual Mediator, others, particularly if they are large with a long contract period or based outside the UK, have a panel. Panels usually comprise of three Mediators, all of whom are well briefed and familiar with the project. So any one of them can be involved at any time. Panels are more difficult to manage as they depend on close communication between the members, but they do allow for a Mentor to be available at any time when an individual member may be unavailable.

Mentors need to engender confidence and trust with everyone involved. So forming good relationships, being seen to be unbiased and non-judgemental, showing experience and wisdom are all important qualities. All are part of being a good and effective Mediator.

Disadvantages:

The advantages of Project Mentoring are obvious – harmonious working relationships, dispute-free, focus on the project, not defending or pursuing claims or fault-finding. It is common sense. However, we are all human and we do not always adopt common sense approaches to life. So the biggest disadvantages to Project

Mentoring are: over-optimism 'this will be a trouble-free project' – is there ever one?; 'we have worked with them before and had no problems' – great, but we are all different and that risks conflict; and late involvement (brought in after the start and when relationships and systems are already in place). And some would consider the involvement of an outsider being an unnecessary expense. The idea of Project Mentoring can be seen to be like an insurance policy – a big premium in anticipation of something going wrong. Preparing for problems may be seen as a sign of weakness. Reputations may be challenged, yet those who have used Project Mentoring will speak of the advantages of working in a collaborative culture where everyone's energy is focussed on the project.

Conclusion:

Project Mentoring is not just for large projects. Snuffing out disputes before they arise has got to be good for any size of project as it preserves working relationships and keeps everyone focussed. It is common knowledge that the alternative – adversarial working attitudes – leads to disputes which are not only costly but are also a diversion of resources and a distraction of focus. Project Mentoring is just plain common sense.

PART 3

Resolving Disputes

In order to effectively resolve disputes the appropriate Dispute Resolution process needs to be chosen and agreed. In order to do that the parties to a dispute need to understand each and every facet to ensure that the process that is utilised is the most suitable to the nature, facts and value of the dispute. There is no 'one size fits all' solution and getting this decision correct from the outset can lead to a quicker, cheaper and more collaborative outcome which, perhaps, can assist in the rebuilding of fractured relationships.

Dispute Resolution has been contained in the lawyers lexicology since the Woolf Reforms and Lord Irvine's ADR pledge around the turn of the last millennium and it began with the calculated move away from the use of departments called 'Commercial Litigation' to 'Commercial Dispute Resolution'. However the subtle reality is that still not enough law firms commit resources to educate their employees and clients in the use of Dispute Resolution let alone Dispute Avoidance or Dispute Management.

Dispute Resolution is the final opportunity for the parties to avoid the gamble and peril of a trial and as such businesses and leaders need to understand what options are available to them and which option might be the most suitable for their needs and their dispute.

The Dispute Resolution landscape & the spectrum of resolution

DISPUTE RESOLUTION SPECTRUM

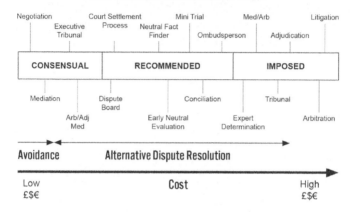

The above spectrum details the landscape of options open to parties who have differences that have escalated into a dispute.

This graphic shows the options, which have been divided into three, often overlapping, types – Consensual (parties find their own solution), Recommended (parties use a third party to advise on a solution) and Imposed (solution imposed by neutral party). The term ADR used to mean Alternative Dispute Resolution, that is alternative to the compulsory processes of Arbitration and litigation (or Adjudication pursuant to the Housing Grants, Construction and Regeneration Act 1996).

Mediation, which is now the main form of ADR, has become so much a part of the UK legal system that it is no longer considered to be alternative. In the UK the courts now expect (that is just short of mandating) parties to consider ADR at some stage of their process and require that the courts be the last resort.

It is not unusual for two (or more) processes to be used in parallel – for example Mediation can take place during an Arbitration or trial and expert opinions (for example on a discrete issue) can be used in many processes in a non-binding way.

The main reason for a party going straight to Arbitration or litigation is ignorance. Once involved, lawyers have a professional responsibility to explain alternative resolution processes, but an informed disputant would already know these processes and only engage a lawyer when other forms have failed.

Choosing the appropriate ADR process & devising creative solutions

The Dispute Resolution spectrum is broad with many methods of Dispute Resolution to choose from. So how do you decide what steps should be taken?

It is in fact not simply a matter of waiting for the dispute to arise. The best time for business parties to decide how to resolve any future disputes, is before they occur as the best way to resolve a dispute is to avoid it in the first place. It is therefore the best advice to think about how you and your counterpart to an agreement will deal with disputes as they arise during the relationship. What is needed is a Dispute Resolution (or multi-tiered Dispute Resolution) clause in the agreement, which provides a road map for the parties when differences arise. This avoids issues over what method to use and it will permit disputes in many cases to be resolved at an early stage.

In most cases, the alternative methods of Dispute Resolution are in fact alternative to litigation. Litigation has been and still is the most common way in which parties will at least commence their way to finding a resolution to their dispute.

> *"I was never ruined but twice:*
> *once when I lost a lawsuit, and once when I won one."*
> Voltaire, 18th Century Enlightenment French Writer

Voltaire's simple statement rings as true today as it did in the 18th century. Litigation in any guise, wherever carried out in the world, rarely brings the benefits sought and often comes at a very high cost. A judicial process, while claiming to ultimately lead to the determination of disputes, usually leaves both the successful party and the losing party dissatisfied. This is because the parties have turned the dispute and the decision over to a third party to judge, based on their findings of fact and determination of the law to be applied. True, the loser can normally appeal, but that only exasperates the cost and extends the time needed for an ultimate determination.

The cost of litigation is not only the costs of the court or arbitral procedure and the lawyers each party must retain. There is a lost opportunity cost that must be added, which includes: business relationships; management and employee time to work on preparing the case, diversion of resources from the business to fighting the legal action, reputational cost that could affect the value of the business. This lost opportunity cost is in fact the most harmful to a business when litigating and speaks to finding alternative ways for dealing with disputes.

There is little question that contentious litigation destroys relationships, robs business of vital resources (be it financial or human capital) and rarely ends with a positive result. A wise business will look for ways to avoid disputes and where that is not possible to mitigate their affect, through strategic use of ADR. This implies finding the appropriate ADR solution to resolving the dispute.

ADR choices can roughly be grouped into those that are meant to prevent disputes from arising (Dispute Avoidance choices) or those that help to manage a dispute and find a resolution after the dispute has arisen (Dispute Management and Resolution choices).

ADR choices:

The choices below have been grouped in accordance with the Dispute Resolution spectrum set out above.

A.   Consensual solution agreed between the parties

Under these ADR mechanisms parties have full control of the process and the neutral is there to facilitate.

1.   Negotiation:

Benjamin Franklin is quoted as having said *"By failing to prepare you are preparing to fail."* It is a trite saying, but too often not heeded. Particularly by lawyers or business people who consider that negotiation is in their blood so why have someone teach them how to do it. But as with anything done well, there are several key factors in setting up an effective negotiation. Michael Leathes in "Negotiation: things corporate counsel need to know but were not taught", summarises them as follows:

- be perceived appropriately by the other party
- understand as much as possible about those you negotiate with
- have the best possible information you can get
- know your real leverage and focus on the other party's
- think carefully about where the other side is coming from
- distinguish between what they want and what they need
- separate fact from fiction and fairness from unreasonableness
- know when to talk and when to walk

- bring your own side along with you
- know where best to turn for support
- be skilled in listening, questioning and deep exploration
- focus and do not let yourself be distracted
- generally, be psyched up for the task

Negotiation between the parties directly or through their advisors is the mechanism by which the vast majority of issues and disputes are resolved. While there is still a relationship between the parties, negotiation is normally successful. As the relationship deteriorates and communications become fraught, direct negotiations lead to failure and the need for a neutral to assist in helping to resolve the dispute becomes necessary.

It is at this point that bringing in a neutral to facilitate the negotiation is an effective tool. Someone who the parties feel is credible and trustworthy, who can help bridge the communication gap, by having them actively listening to each other's needs, rather than simply arguing about their rights. This need not yet be a Mediator, but simply a trusted neutral.

2.   Mediation:

Mediation is a Dispute Resolution method that can be used at any time to attempt resolution of disputes. No formal process or steps need have been taken and so Mediation can be seen either as a Dispute Avoidance mechanism, dealing with a conflict before it becomes a dispute,, or as a Dispute Management and or Resolution tool to be used once a formal dispute has arisen.

As previously set out in this Guide, Mediation can be built into the Dispute Resolution clause of an agreement, as a formal step to be used after attempts at negotiation between the parties have failed and the use of a neutral to assist the parties is seen as beneficial, but before other formal steps such as Arbitration or litigation may be commenced.

Mediation can also be built into formal relationships that require conflicts which arise to be dealt with quickly and inexpensively, so that the object of the agreement can be carried out. Project Mediation, much like Dispute Boards, can be used on long term projects and joint ventures to mitigate the risk of relationships failing and contracts not being completed.

The primary benefits of using Mediation are:

- Mediation is a consensual process that parties can contractually agree to utilise
- The Mediator has no power to bind the parties. Instead, he or she serves as an objective facilitator
- Discussions with the Mediator are confidential and without prejudice to encourage the parties to be candid about strengths and weaknesses
- Mediations are held in an informal setting, usually over a one to three-day period. Each party is required to bring a person with settlement authority

Mediation offers numerous advantages over other forms of Dispute Resolution:

- Parties decide how their dispute is to be resolved rather than having it decided for them by a third party

- Helps to preserve relationships by permitting parties to resolve issues early on, keeping open channels of communication that would normally be damaged or destroyed through litigation
- Business management gets involved in the settlement process at an early stage
- Experienced Mediators facilitate negotiations, minimise posturing by overzealous advocates and provide reality checks on strengths and weaknesses
- Allows parties to explore interests and not simply legal rights
- Tends to be cheaper and faster than litigation or Arbitration, in particular reducing lost opportunity costs
- Permits international parties to cross cultural barriers
- Process is flexible, giving the parties the ability to structure the format in the way they believe most conducive to reaching resolution
- Voluntary settlements substantially reduce the risk that one party will seek to set aside the resolution, such as occurs with appeals from court orders or motions to vacate Arbitration awards.

3. Executive Tribunal:

A hybrid form of Mediation where the Mediator sits with an executive / decision-maker from each / all side(s). The Mediator hears the case presentations and then leads a negotiation between the parties. The Mediator chairs the opening session, then assists the negotiation in a similar way to a conventional Mediation although often, being a small group, everyone stays together. This is not a common form of Mediation but, for example, it has been successfully used in the motor industry.

4.   Arb / Med & Adj / Med:

These do not sit easily in the 'Consensual' section as they result from a formal, law-bound imposed decision process that changes at the end into a Mediation. Many Arbitrators and Adjudicators have also been trained as Mediators and, with suitable cases, sometimes offer to mediate a settlement rather than impose a decision on the parties. By implication this means that the Arbitration or Adjudication process is well under way, if not complete, and so the full (and rarely small) cost will already have been incurred. Usually the Arbitrator or Adjudicator will have made their decision, but, by agreement, it is not revealed unless the Mediation is unsuccessful. It does give the parties the opportunity, given what has been said during the hearing(s), to determine their own outcome rather than have one imposed upon them. The Arbitrator / Adjudicator can only make a decision according to the relevant law and contract, whereas, in the Mediation, the parties can do whatever deal they wish (so long as it is legal). However, it does beg the question as to why go to the expense of the Arbitration or Adjudication to have a Mediation at the end when they could have had a much quicker and cheaper process in having a Mediation in the first place.

B.   Recommended (but not imposed) solution to the dispute

Under these ADR processes the neutral provides a non-binding recommendation.

1.   Dispute Boards or Conflict Avoidance Boards:

These boards have traditionally been used in construction projects and are a contractual mechanism, but now expanding into any long term relationships. Usually built into the contract from the outset, these boards are generally composed of one or three neutrals having the required expertise needed by the project. The parties are meant to include the board in project meetings and to discuss issues with it, as they arise. Depending on the type of board chosen, a non-binding or binding determination is rendered to resolve the matter, often before it becomes an ingrained dispute. The strength of the process is that it allows issues to be spotted early and before they become disputes and thus is a true Dispute Avoidance mechanism.

When a non-binding recommendation is issued, the role of the board is not to impose a decision but to provide the parties with a means to resolve their dispute. Not being imposed, the parties are free not to adopt it. Where the role of the board is adjudicative, the board falls into the category of imposing a decision on the parties. In that case, the parties must continue performance pending litigation or Arbitration. In fact, most decisions are not contested.

This is a good mechanism to build into long term contracts, for projects that are technical in nature and that require the parties to continue performance, while disputes are dealt with separately. It is effective when the parties choose board members with the experience and credibility to be listened to and whose advice or decision, will be accepted. The board should also be part of the project right from the outset and not only when disputes arise.

2.   Court settlement process:

This process probably sits on the cusp of 'Consensual' and 'Recommended' sections. In theory it is a form of Mediation, hence being in the former section. However, it is greatly influenced by the 'Mediator' and so could easily be seen as consultative, in other words, using a third party to advise on a solution. In 2006 the Technology and Construction Court in the UK devised an 'informal' but confidential settlement process whereby a judge holds settlement discussions with the parties in the hope of brokering a deal. Of course, the judge is influenced by his / her opinion of the likely outcome if the matter went to trial, and indeed may well give an opinion during the discussions and so influence the parties' legal position. But it is assumed that the judge is impartial and has a role purely to broker discussions, do some serious reality testing but not to influence the outcome. If settlement does not occur, the judge may be asked for a written opinion (which would be non-binding) and of course that may carry significant weight in further negotiations, probably more so than any counsel's or expert's opinion.

The scheme has not been used a great deal and stories circulate about the judge only seeing the lawyers, not the parties themselves. So it is far from a party-focused Mediation but does at least offer the chance to avoid a costly (in money, time and emotion) trial.

The judge is, of course, precluded from sitting if the matter does not settle and so goes to court.

3.   Neutral Fact Finder:

The parties' disagreement may be over certain facts or technicalities and they may choose to use a jointly-appointed neutral, usually an expert, to research and report on such discrete issues. Any recommendation would be non-binding. This in itself may resolve the differences or it may, more usually, be done as part of a resolution process such as Mediation, to clarify particular issues.

4.   Early Neutral Evaluation ("ENE"):

Sometimes termed 'Judicial Review', ENE involves a jointly-appointed neutral (usually a retired judge) reviewing the facts and relevant law and forming a (non-binding) opinion on the likely outcome if the case went to court. This would normally involve a significant amount of reading of documents and so would not be a cheap process although it has the benefit over counsel's opinion in that the neutral is jointly appointed and therefore jointly instructed. This avoids the problem with each party instructing their own counsel and, because of different instructions, giving different, often conflicting, opinions.

This mechanism is useful where the parties are entrenched with respect to liability and valuation issues. One party may have conceded liability but disagrees on the level of damages claimed. A respected neutral can in such cases often render an opinion that the parties will accept, due to that neutral's prior experience. Before agreeing to settle, parties often want to know how strong their case is and this mechanism allows them to explore that.

5.   **Mini Trial:**

This is a method of resolution, which aims to find a commercial rather than legal solution to the dispute. It is also a non-binding process. The parties each select a representative to a tribunal and a neutral is selected as the chair. A brief presentation, which is strictly limited in content and length is then made to the tribunal, after which the tribunal confers. The strength of the process is in the fact that the party representatives come to have a better understanding of the other party's position and the neutral can play a role, much as a Mediator in helping to reality check positions. A resolution is not limited to the facts before the tribunal and a settlement can encompass many different business considerations.

This mechanism is a variation on having a Mediation. It allows the parties to make a more structured submission to the tribunal. The fact that there is a neutral involved helps the discussion to move from positional negotiation to an exploration of interests and needs. While not used very often, it has its place where parties are still relatively cooperative and genuinely looking for ways to resolve a dispute amicably.

6.   **Conciliation:**

Conciliation is now commonly accepted as a form of Mediation which provides for the Mediator facilitating a settlement between the parties, but failing that making a decision (which, by prior agreement, is usually binding unless overturned by the courts or Arbitrator) if the parties do not reach a joint agreement. It is used in some engineering contracts and workplace disputes. Its advantage is that it gives finality, whether consensual or not. The main disadvantage is that the parties may be careful about the information given to the Mediator and so withhold sensitive, even damaging information that would otherwise have aided a settlement.

7.   Ombudsperson:

Ombudsperson programmes have widely been used by companies to deal with both internal and external issues that arise from time to time, enabling a third party to discuss matters with the parties on a confidential basis. Ombudspersons generally make recommendations on how the problem can be resolved, but it is up to the parties to decide whether to accept them or not. This tool is often seen in business / consumer matters or employee issues within a company. It can be effective if the parties have confidence that the Ombudsperson is truly neutral and where problems can be discussed at an early stage. Parties are generally free to proceed to raise the dispute to a further legal stage if the Ombudsperson process fails to resolve the matter.

This is a good mechanism for maintaining ongoing relationships, be they within or outside of the business and demonstrates to employees and customers that a Company has a process in place to deal with complaints.

C.   Imposed outcome to the dispute (where a third party decides)

Under these ADR processes, parties turn the dispute over to neutrals to impose a binding decision.

1.   Expert Determination:

This is often used when the parties have an impasse that requires a neutral expert to use their expertise to review the matter in dispute and provide an expert opinion. For example, in a building dispute about the quality of steel used in meeting the specification, an engineer expert in steel production could review the material used and render an opinion as to its quality. The opinion can be binding or non-binding on the parties, although in many jurisdictions there is legislation that covers expert opinions and deals with the process and effect of an expert opinion.

This is an effective mechanism, where there is a technical matter at issue that an expert can provide an opinion on, that the parties will accept and move on. The risk is that where the opinion is legally binding, the parties must be confident in both the process and the expert as they will be stuck with it.

2.   Med / Arb:

This is a hybrid process by which the parties agree to engage in Mediation, with the intention of submitting all unresolved issues to final and binding Arbitration. It is usually advised that the Arbitrator should not be the same person who served as the Mediator. The reason being, that parties will reveal information in Mediation which is meant to remain confidential. It will be difficult for the Arbitrator not to be biased once confidential information is known, which is an essential characteristic for an Arbitrator to have.

This is a mechanism often used in multi-tiered Dispute Resolution clauses, where the dispute is elevated from one ADR mechanism to the next, to find the appropriate one to resolve the dispute. Given that Mediation is becoming more commonly used in most commercial disputes at some point in the Dispute Resolution process, it is natural to include it before Arbitration in a Dispute Resolution clause.

This is a good process to use where the parties wish to have a mechanism that first attempts to find a consensual resolution through a neutral Mediator, but failing this, in order to have finality, the process moves on to a binding mechanism, in this case Arbitration. This is a good solution to use on projects or agreements where there is a long term relationship that has to be maintained, ultimately to deliver the objective of the agreement.

3.   Tribunal:

Tribunals are most common in the UK where they are government appointed and lay down binding legal decisions. Tribunals cover a broad range of areas, including land and property disputes, employment disputes dealing with discrimination, dismissal, bullying, harassment and so on; the Health Service, dealing with care standards, mental health issues; immigration, asylum and asylum support. They are also established in other sectors, particularly in the sports sector and comprise a panel of three people, one of whom is Chair.

4.   Adjudication:

Adjudication is the commonly adopted form of Dispute Resolution in the UK construction industry (where it is a statutory right under the Housing Grants, Construction and Regeneration Act 1996) although it is generally available in any sector. It is a legal process and the law and practice of Adjudication has developed and become more detailed, and therefore more complicated and protracted.

Nowadays it is rarely a quick and cheap route to resolution as awards might need to be enforced by the courts and the Adjudicator's decision can sometimes be appealed and overturned by an Arbitrator, so, although the parties act on the Adjudicator's decisions during the currency of the contract, those decisions can be ratified or reversed through Arbitration at the end.

5.   Arbitration:

Arbitration is typically the ultimate Dispute Resolution method chosen by parties from different jurisdictions contracting with each other. This is largely because neither party wants to give the other 'home court advantage'. Some of the considerations to consider when deciding whether Arbitration or litigation is to be chosen in the disputes clause are described below.

Arbitration versus litigation – issues to consider:

- Does Arbitration provide a safer alternative than a foreign judicial system? Is a foreign court system expeditious, trustworthy, reliable and fair?

- Does Arbitration provide demonstrable cost and time savings over litigation in foreign courts?
- Does litigation provide surer means to enforce the outcome (judgment versus award)?
- How does each forum handle discovery and disclosure issues?
- Would a dispute process benefit from expertise in the decision-maker?
- Is the subject matter of the transaction one that would benefit from a private, as opposed to public, Dispute Resolution process?
- Are there any local law requirements or constraints?

The key characteristics of Arbitration are the following:

- Agreement to resolve disputes privately outside the framework of national courts. It requires a written Arbitration agreement (can be in the main contract or in a side agreement) between the parties
- The parties determine the mechanism pursuant to which the Arbitration will be carried out, e.g., whether it will be ad hoc or institutional (using the rules of an existing arbitral institution)
- Arbitration is conducted by a Tribunal normally consisting of one to three Arbitrators
- Arbitration results in a final, binding and enforceable determination of the parties' rights and obligations in the form of an award

Arbitration is a good solution as the ultimate tool where other ADR mechanisms have been considered or have failed. Where there is an intractable dispute that simply cannot be resolved, or matters in contention have been narrowed, Arbitration provides the parties with a relatively quick, binding and enforceable award.

6.   Litigation (not seen as an alternative but mainstream)

Similar to Arbitration, a judge sits in court, hears the legal arguments and witness statements and decides who is right (or more right) and who is wrong. It results in a winner and a loser (who usually pays the majority of the costs of both sides' legal team) and can only really award financial damages or grant an injunction. Whether it be the establishment of ADR or the introduction of almost punitive court fees or the almost non-existence of legal aid, the wish for courts to be the last resort has been largely achieved. Most people see the courts as something to be avoided. Those who have not avoided them usually wish never to repeat the experience as Voltaire attests to. It is a costly experience in emotion, finance and time.

Conclusion:

- There are a broad range of Dispute Resolution mechanisms to choose from
- These reflect the parties' choice as to whether to emphasise Dispute Avoidance, Dispute Management and Resolution or imposed finality
- Careful consideration should be given to which mechanism or range of mechanisms to employ depending on questions of relationships, cost, time and finality

- Ultimately the mechanism(s) chosen should be tailored to the nature of the agreement being entered into by the parties (not simply boiler plate) or the type of dispute that has arisen.

It's all about relationships, relationships & relationships

A focus on relationships will help businesses avoid, manage and resolve their disputes.

This Guide has drawn compelling insights from the experiences of The DARP's team across a rich tapestry of challenges in business, society and the world generally. What lessons can be learnt and how can these be applied in the business relationships that occur on a day-to-day basis to deliver a more positive and productive outcome?

Our perspectives on traditional ways of managing issues in dispute:

The DARP passionately believes that the challenges we face in business, in society, and between governments could be much more productively dealt with if more time is spent on focusing on the relationships between the parties, as an enabler to resolving the issues in dispute.

Furthermore, even though The DARP expound the virtue and value of Mediation (in particular) to avoid, manage and resolve disputes it is an accepted fact that parties who take disputes all the way to court rarely leave satisfied.

David Evans commented directly on this specific point:

"I decided after several years to stop practising commercial Mediation – I was frustrated that, even though it is the enlightened parties who take the Mediation route, commercial Mediations often left a feeling of dissatisfaction at the end of a successful settlement. Both sides would only focus on the immediate issues in dispute, and would reach a settlement late in the day, often after much posturing. I still remember the Mediation where a client and his lawyer stood with their coats on whilst holding the door handle for two hours and threatening to leave, before we reached agreement! Both parties would then shake hands before departing, determined never to do business together again. I decided instead to focus on relationship breakdowns where there is a continuing need for the parties to work together after the Mediation, such as Mediation between company directors or partnerships".

Oliver was asked how he approaches the perceived dissatisfaction with a non-relationship focused outcome "One of the early phrases that I grew up with was the notion of 'shared pain' and how both parties, or all parties in the case of a multi-party matter, conclude their dispute having neither won nor lost and knowing that they have suffered – the suffering is almost always a financial impediment. The issue with this accepted principle of a satisfactory Mediation is that these feelings of annoyance, or dispiritedness rarely engender a positive end. A Mediation post-issue (by that I mean a Mediation that has been convened or sometimes even court ordered, after parties to the dispute have already become embroiled in a formal legal battle) does not often, and in fact very rarely indeed, result in a future relationship being protected. The simple truth of the reason behind this is due to the costs and adversarial nature of the process that the parties have to endure to get there.

A pre-action Mediation (one that occurs before the formal Claim Form has been issued at court) provides the parties with the ideal opportunity to resolve their dispute before legal costs become a barrier to settlement and positions have become so entrenched that the 'no-man's land' between them becomes too impenetrable. The earlier the use of Mediation the better as the size of the 'dispute gap' is naturally far smaller than months later and therefore the opportunity for a collaboratively focused outcome is greater as is the prospect of a future relationship being preserved".

When David Richbell was asked in 2018 about his thoughts about preservation of relationships he commented that "I often feel a tinge of disappointment at the lack of focus in restoring relationships in disputes, and where the opportunity to turn over a new page is not taken. It is of course true that most parties who end up going to court do not want to repeat the process, but it is still a challenge to encourage parties to rebuild relationships. My feeling is that parties in commercial disputes can learn from transformative Mediation, for example in the community, where there is a focus on relationships. Often in commercial discussions the focus is on problem solving, money and a deal, even if individuals are hurting".

The Church of England and women priests:

David Richbell was heavily involved in the conferences regarding the introduction of women priests into the Church of England and in respect of the difficulties faced in addressing the dynamics of this type of relationship David remarked that "On 12 March 1994, the first 32 women were ordained as Church of England priests. For five years before that I facilitated a series of discussions between the two opposing sides in the Church of England to find common ground and a way forward on the issue of admitting women to the priesthood. When dealing with people with strong religious beliefs I found that this often prevented rational conversations, as individuals feel their core beliefs are being challenged, and as a result can adopt very defensive positions. This is equivalent in some respects to individuals in commercial Mediations saying, 'this is a matter of 'principle'".

The lessons that David was able to learn from the facilitative discussions regarding women priests were:

- Time can heal – often in business we regard lengthy delays negatively and as prevarication. Discussing really emotional issues over a lengthy period can often help create the conditions for the parties to establish an effective dialogue, and to work together, with trust rebuilding slowly
- Broken trust cannot be rebuilt quickly – much effort has to be spent on creating a willingness to move on, and perhaps forgiveness follows later. This is similar to the process in Workplace Mediation where the starting point for discussions is often the complete breakdown of trust, and the outcome of the Mediation is simply a willingness to tentatively work together, not a complete transformation of relationships and the re-establishment of full trust in each other
- The Church of England had come so close to a cataclysmic schism on a number of occasions during these facilitated discussions, with the group who were anti-women priests threatening to leave the Church. Yet years later the change

has happened and the vast majority of Church of England bishops, clergy, laity and parishioners welcome women priests as the 'status quo'.

The Northern Ireland peace process:

David Evans, in his discussions with David Richbell in 2018, reflected on the Northern Ireland peace process and observed that the Northern Ireland peace process had run for several years before April 1998, when the Good Friday Agreement was signed by the different political factions in Northern Ireland, and the British and Irish governments. Over 3,600 people were killed and thousands more injured during 30 years of inter communal conflict between the Protestant / Loyalist and Roman Catholic / Nationalist communities during what was understatedly called "The Troubles". In recent years the homicide rate in Northern Ireland has reduced by 97% to 0.9 per 100,000 inhabitants per year. This is a similar murder rate to the UK, the Republic of Ireland, and most Western European nations, regions which have among the lowest homicide rates globally. During The Troubles, homicide rates were considerably higher: at their height in 1972 there were 479 deaths caused either by paramilitary or Security Forces' action – a rate of 31 per 100,000 inhabitants.

The Northern Ireland peace process is regarded as a tremendous achievement, and in stark contrast to the lack of progress in resolving other intractable inter-communal conflicts elsewhere in the world, for example Syria, Palestine / Israel. However more than twenty years after the Belfast Agreement there are still a number of festering issues of tension and mistrust between the two communities:

- Belfast still has many "peace walls", crude and ugly walls which separate adjoining Catholic / Nationalist and Protestant / Loyalist neighbourhoods
- Teenagers who were born after the Belfast Agreement take part in ritual rioting
- Mental health issues are significantly higher in Northern Ireland than elsewhere in western Europe
- A significant majority of children continue to be educated separately, based on religion
- Paramilitary organisations continue to operate in the background; and most importantly, politics in Northern Ireland is still dominated by tribal rivalry between the two communities
- The power sharing arrangements agreed in the Belfast Agreement did not operate between January 2017 and January 2020 due to a breakdown in trust between the two main political parties.

David Evans considers that "It may be time now for Northern Ireland to benefit from a second wave of conflict resolution, based on a mature recognition that the first intervention in the form of the Belfast Agreement was a major step forward but was by necessity the best agreement that could be reached at that time. With twenty plus years of hindsight there is an argument for addressing the remaining issues which divide the two communities, such as: the continuing education of the children based on sectarian lines; and the continuing inability of thousands of the victims of violence to obtain closure due to the fact that very few individuals are pursued through the criminal justice system, and no mechanism such as a "truth and reconciliation" commission was implemented to enable victims to obtain restorative justice, for example by hearing directly from those who perpetrated violence against their relatives. How can an individual move on when they have a burning sense of injustice and hurt dominating all their thoughts and feelings?

Furthermore it may be time to recognise that, as in any business or government organisation, there may be a need for structural change to the original solution in order to reflect changing needs. Does it still make sense for the political governance structure to reflect the division between the two communities, as opposed to what brings them together?"

David was struck by a quote in Robert Key's *A History of Ireland* in the late 1970s where a Protestant woman said, *"I feel sorry for the Catholics because they are living in darkness"*. And what did a Catholic woman say? - *"I feel sorry for the Protestants because they are living in darkness"*. Representatives of the two communities were united in their ignorance and hatred of each other. Could there be a better way forward, based on the proposition that maybe both communities can be right, instead of one having to be right and the other automatically wrong? How would such a different approach manifest itself in Northern Ireland?

One example of how such an approach could work would be in the establishment of a "Living Museum of The Troubles" where visitors would visit both sides of a peace wall to hear both the Protestant / loyalist and the Catholic / Nationalist perspective on different days in history. It would be enlightening to hear the different perspectives on the day civil rights marches started in 1969, or the day the Irish Republican Army ("IRA") nearly succeeded in killing the British

Prime Minister in the Brighton bomb.

The insights that might apply to the business world which we can draw from the negotiations resulting in the Belfast Agreement, and the improved but not perfect situation many years later are:

- An imperfect solution can be good enough to enable a really intractable problem to be stabilised and improve
- Don't leave a solution entombed in concrete – have the courage to recognise that we may need to revisit the solution at a later point in order to move in stages to ever higher plateaux
- The original Belfast Agreement required considerable compromise on all sides. Indeed several of the main political leaders who took the really brave decisions to compromise were later swept from office by their electorates. Maybe real leaders of vision realise that, in order to make a breakthrough in an otherwise completely intractable position, they have to make decisions which they know will be very difficult to push through internally within their support base, and which may come at personal cost to the leader
- Lastly and most importantly, the breakthroughs that took place which enabled sworn enemies to sit down together in government, were only possible because the facilitators of the peace process took the time to enable the opposing parties to begin to build relationships between them. To see one's implacable opponent as a human being, and furthermore to understand their humanity, can enable the most momentous of changes in mindset to occur. Such an approach would probably have produced a different solution to the UK's Brexit crisis.

The importance of relationships, a post 9/11 example:

Wolf, reflecting on David Evans' experiences of Northern Ireland, considered an instance of effective relationship management following the 9/11 terrorist attack:

"One of the painful learning points from 9/11, which was acutely apparent in New York City, was that the different emergency services could not communicate directly with each other on the day of the attacks on the World Trade Centre towers. They were all on different wireless systems, and New York's skyscraper topography did not help. Northrop Grumman Corporation ("NGC") were asked by the City of New York to develop systems which would enable communication between the emergency services. This was a very high profile request and they had to deliver.

NGC's solution utilised technology from other companies under licence. One of the technologies used by NGC was from a South Korean software supplier, where NGC believed they had an existing licence agreement which would cover their needs. A dispute arose as the South Korean software supplier felt the previous licence agreement did not extend to the use to which NGC wanted for the technology.

NGC was on a very tight schedule to deliver the solution and could not afford a lengthy delay due to negotiation and litigation. The Korean company threatened to secure an injunction preventing NGC from using its software. A commercial Mediation was duly organised and NGC's CEO decided to attend in person. The Korean company was much smaller and the attendance of NGC's CEO indicated how seriously NGC took the issue. Therefore both NGC's CEO and the Korean company's President attended the Mediation.

At the Mediation NGC's CEO apologised to the President of the Korean company – he was sorry the President felt that NGC was misappropriating the technology covered by the previous licence agreement, but he recognised the Korean company felt differently. NGC's CEO recognised that the relationship between their two companies was important going forward. The outcome of the Mediation was the two companies agreed to implement a new licence agreement which would also cover other projects.

NGC's CEO apologising in the Mediation was the recognition of the value of focusing on relationships in a commercial context. This focus enabled a transformation of the two parties' relationships to allow business to continue and develop. The Mediation enabled the two companies to reach a new agreement on future royalty payments, as opposed to looking back on perceived losses. In effect the apology was effective in allowing the parties to put the past aside and be willing to look forward.

The importance of recognising the need for strong relationships, backed up by an understanding of each party's cultural requirements, is particularly important in commercial arrangements which operate across borders, such as the cross border automotive and communication industries. These industries have large and complex supply chains, with hosts of prime and sub-contract suppliers, and where parties often need to be pre-qualified to appear in the supply chain. Therefore there are a limited number of parties to deal with – if they fall out there is a very long process to replace a party. In reality companies operating in this context cannot afford to fall out so they build in robust Mediation provisions to resolve conflict as soon as possible. In the North American Free Trade Agreement ("NAFTA") context it could take ten to twenty years to replace sub-contract infrastructure so there is a compelling need for non-adversarial relationships.

In long term supply arrangements the parties often need to continue serving each other on associated contracts or under long term contracts, long after they have experienced a dispute on one of their contracts. The maintenance of relationships on long term contracts, or the rebuilding of fractured relationships, can require extensive and repeated efforts by senior management. In order to achieve a continuing relationship parties in these circumstances often invest considerable amounts of time to focus on relationships through mechanisms such as a Dispute Board (often found on government contracts or large construction projects) or in a Project Mediator.

Dispute Boards typically have three members – a legally qualified Chair, and two independent members, such as engineers, who are familiar with the contract or the project, and can be set up in various forms, including working on an informal basis (providing a non-binding opinion) or providing an interim binding determination.

What inferences can we draw for business in general?

There is value in focusing on relationships outside the particular scenario of long term contracts. If companies and organisations can use relationships to reduce and resolve conflict because they have no choice other than to maintain the relationship, how much better would businesses operate if commercial parties consistently invested in establishing and maintaining excellent relationships?

Disputes are extremely costly when they result in litigation with unsatisfactory outcomes in the form of costs, internal disruption, stress, and distracted management. Mechanisms that foster good relationships and which can prevent conflict from arising or resolve conflict as soon as practicable after it arises, make good business sense".

Societal tensions and extremism:

When Zaza first started mediating in 2006, she undertook Commercial, Matrimonial, Medical and Workplace Mediation. During 2013 to 2019, Zaza refocussed her attention on Mediation within families and between community groups in London and Kent rather than commercial Mediation. Referrals included: Parents who had lost hope in a child due to clashes between East-West norms; tensions and conflict between individuals and groups from the extreme right and mosques; and counter-radicalisation measures with prisoners from Muslim groups.

Zaza recounted an example of a seemingly irreconcilable rift that had developed between a 15 year old boy and his mother. Local stakeholder agencies asked Zaza to work with the boy because he had recently been expelled from school, was known to engage in criminality and they feared he was also becoming increasingly immersed in radical Islamic extremism.

When Zaza first met with both of them at his mother's home she could see the objectionable way he spoke to his mother, openly rebuking her about not asking him if he wanted her to make him tea too. The mother explained that she had sent her son to her family in Pakistan when he was 13 to put a distance between him and some young men in his locality in the UK because she feared that he was drifting towards criminality. She added that their relationship had been fraught with difficulties since his return and that he had occasionally physically assaulted her too.

The boy eventually confided in Zaza that he deeply resented his mother for *"abandoning me in Pakistan which is a foreign country to me! She just p****d off back to the UK and forced me to live with family members I've never met before."* The boy said that he was *"pitied"* by his Pakistani cousins who called him *"a reject,"* and so he spent most of his time in the village mosque where he made friends *"with some young brothers (men) who spoke the truth".* He also complained vehemently about his mother engaging with the "kufaar" (non-believers) stakeholders in the UK and trying to control him.

Zaza met with the boy seven times and worked through the same phases of Dispute Resolution which a commercial Mediator would do with the parties to a commercial dispute, such as: listening attentively, exploring the deeper layers of conflict, reframing vitriolic statements, building rapport and trust, to identify and unlock the core of the conflict and resentment.

Zaza explored with the boy where his behaviour might ultimately lead, and initially he scoffed about the likely impact of ending up in prison. So Zaza took him on a visit to a prison and he was petrified.

This reality test was his turning point. In order to start to make progress with him it took a Mediator to show an interest in him as an individual and explore what was really behind his posturing, followed by some completely candid reality testing, to help him move to a position where he could make an informed choice about his way forward.

This work has now been extended formally into a programme where radicalised (right wing and Islamist) prisoners receive mentoring support as an integral part of their licence conditions. The aim of this work is to support their resettlement in the community by providing a positive purpose in their lives, in order to prevent them from falling back under the influence of the radicalisers. This work involves showing an interest in the individual as a person (often the only other person to do this is the radicaliser), humanising them by building a strong rapport with them, and reality testing them on their ideological and theological beliefs.

Some aspects of relationship building are particularly important in order to make progress with someone who holds deeply entrenched beliefs. Central to building rapport is to make them feel valued as a human being, rather than just focusing on an issue. This focus on the person rather than the task is probably not the order in which many business people or indeed Mediators address the resolution of a problem.

A further nuance in the approach when dealing with radicalised people is to address the relationship issues he/she has within themselves, as well as addressing relationship issues between people. Relationship issues we have within ourselves are typically difficult to address in Western culture. For example, in performance management discussions with an employee, who is clearly struggling in work, we tend to shy away from 'getting personal' with the individual. This is especially so when dealing with concepts such as shame.

Zaza explained that she always drills down in discussion to understand how mentees or parties in the Mediation see themselves. All too often lurking beneath the overt defensiveness is a lot of shame.

An example of where this may be a factor is where some ethnic minority families in the UK resort to violence when their daughter's conduct has deviated from their parents' acceptable norms: such as having a boyfriend. The father may say *"I don't have a daughter of that name – she is dead to me"*. Giving the father the opportunity to acknowledge his shame about the breach of trust in his relationship with his daughter's action and his objectionable and destructive reaction can be a cathartic release that will not restore his dignity but will significantly reduce his shame.

In applying these insights to the commercial world we often see situations where both sides hold deeply entrenched positions, putting blame on someone else, and we often do not get to the point where we enable a party to step out of their deeply entrenched position. A lot of conflict focuses on how others see us rather than how we see ourselves, and we can miss the opportunity to see how a party to a dispute can reflect further and change their position.

From Zaza's viewpoint and experience the focus on exploring the mutual needs (met and unmet) that are an imperative part of a relationship in the context of their cultural identities, is critical to the healing process. Zaza advises that in the commercial world, we should not just hurriedly focus on resolving the immediate dispute, without exploring the possibilities for facilitating an improved understanding of each party (or parties) cultural identity needs.

Final Thoughts

When all is said and done that which was said and done still remains.

The need to win or to be proved right for yourself, your company or your peers can, and often does, impact on the future in a negative way. Positive relationships and effective lines of communication can be damaged beyond repair during the 'heat of the battle'. Too often have litigants declared that *"I'll never do business with them ever again"* or *"I'll never talk to that person again"*. The polarisation of viewpoints or legal arguments or even the stances adopted by lawyers will always widen the 'dispute gap' but if the parties accept that their actions, attitude and approach could dramatically transform the dispute into one that is avoidable, manageable or resolvable in the first place then the outcome will be achieved in a more cost effective and harmonious way. This can only offer a greater opportunity for the relationship to continue.

When arguments, disagreements or disputes first erupt, like the volcano spewing out the molten lava of vitriol, and if the parties had sight of this Guide or had the understanding to communicate effectively, the consequences would not be the inevitable disaster that was not foreseen or protected against.

The desire to claw back what was said or what was done is a natural (but often very private) emotional reaction to a dispute especially when the dispute gap has widened because of it. *"I wished I never had started this"* is a commonplace sentiment during the rigours of litigation but actually *"with hindsight I'd have done things differently"* applies more readily to all forms of disputes and not just legal cases as there is often a mere handful of events, statements or actions, or even just a solitary one, that created the volcanic eruption and it is impossible to stop it once it has happened.

The Volcano Insurance that The DARP are suggesting in this Guide is intended to assist switched on leaders to understand that there are processes and options in place to both prevent conflict and protect communication and relationships ideally before eruption but if need be after as well.

Everything, when all is said and done, is about relationships and how a positive one will create an atmosphere of collaboration and facilitation even when a dispute arises.

My father, David Richbell, would often declare that *"you work with what you've got"* and if this Guide achieves its aim it will be that if you've got a relationship based on collaboration, facilitation and understanding then communication will be easier, even if difficult conversations are required, thereby reducing risk and saving time and money.

The DARP and this Guide therefore offers Volcano Insurance for the benefit of hindsight beforehand.

Oliver Richbell
Partner, The Dispute Avoidance & Resolution Partnership

THE DARP PARTNERS
& CONSULTANTS

David A Evans brings over 30 years experience in executive business leadership and Mediation. His main area of interest is in the prevention and resolution of conflict where the parties need to maintain an effective working relationship. David is an accredited CEDR Mediator and sits on the Executive and workplace panel of the specialist Mediation chambers *IPOS*. David founded The Diversity & Innovation Company whose purpose is to bring diversity of thought into the heart and soul of business. It sends business leaders on real life experiences with Indian schools, to help them develop their emotional intelligence.

David Richbell was a founding partner of The Dispute Avoidance & Resolution Partnership and one of the world's most experienced and respected commercial Mediators. David was continuously acknowledged by the leading legal directories including in 2014 when he was recognised by 'Who's Who Legal' as "one of the most respected commercial Mediators in the world" and in 2016 as a "Thought Leader in Mediation". David was also arguably the finest trainer of mediators there has ever been and he also wrote many articles and books but his "Mediation of Construction Disputes" and "How to Master Commercial Mediation" remain a go to for business leaders and Mediators across the world.

David passed away in September 2018 leaving an enduring legacy of respect, achievement and love.

Ian White has been the chief legal officer and company secretary for both listed and major private companies. While Ian spent most of his career as a lawyer, he also spent some time working as a strategy consultant. Ian now works as a consultant, coach, trainer and facilitator. Ian's previous experience led him to develop an expertise in corporate governance and working with boards on effectiveness, enhancement and performance. Ian also works with directors and lawyers on training and development. Ian undertakes assignments in the not-for-profit and public sectors. As well as being a lawyer Ian has an MBA from Ashridge Business School, a coaching qualification, and is also a *CEDR* (Centre for Effective Dispute Resolution) accredited Mediator and he is also currently training in how to assess psychometric questionnaires.

Oliver Richbell is a founding Partner of The Dispute Avoidance & Resolution Partnership and a former commercial litigation solicitor. He now applies his years of experience to assist businesses to avoid disputes where possible, or to manage them pragmatically, or to resolve them in the most commercial way. His approach of placing the client's interests as his paramount objective leads to the greater use of facilitation and collaborative processes in the formation, preparation, drafting and reviewing of commercial agreements therefore reducing the possibility of disputes occurring at all. Oliver passionately believes that effective, efficient and client engaged contract formulation is the root of successful Dispute Avoidance. Oliver also applies the principles of collaborative working and facilitation to assist businesses to manage and resolve their disputes as quickly and as cost effectively as possible.

Stephen Hall is a former head of marketing and communications at Ericsson and has worked across Europe, Middle East, Asia and USA, providing a breadth of customer and company experience. He has in depth knowledge of company operations in the legal, employee, pension, tax and co-determination aspects which allows him to create innovative solutions to conflict situations. He mediates, consults in areas including strategy, provides leadership development and carries a heart of peacebuilding.

Wolf von Kumberg brings over 30 years of International legal and business experience to the practice of ADR having served as Legal Director and Assistant General Counsel to Northrop Grumman Corporation and before that to Litton Industries Inc. He is now applying this accumulated knowledge to the field of global commercial conflict avoidance and resolution as a Mediator, Arbitrator and Dispute Board member with offices in both London and Washington DC.

Dr Zaza Johnson Elsheikh is dually qualified as a medical doctor and solicitor as well as being a highly experienced Mediator and International Commercial Arbitrator (CIArb). She is an active pluralist and fluent in Arabic. Zaza frequently contributes to the prevention of and response to radicalisation through Mediation and mentoring, often working alongside the Metropolitan Police. As a Conflict Resolution trainer, restorative justice practitioner and community leader for Muslim women, Zaza also delivers a range of courses and seminars in Churches, Mosques, Schools and Universities as well teaching children (including those with Special Educational Needs) to handle conflicts with their peers, siblings and parents more constructively. Her commitment to improving the levels of engagement within ethnic and religious communities is strongly evidenced by her founding of the charity *BIMA*, a multi-faith association of Mediators and Arbitrators.

DEDICATION

When people ask me to talk about my father David Richbell and what he meant to me there is always a pause for reflection and contemplation. The silence is not intentional and there is no need for me to search for the words it is just how do you encapsulate a lifetime of love into a few sentences?

David is the greatest man that I will ever meet and in 2015 when we jointly created The DARP it was the perfect moment for us to come together and embark on a business that we are so passionate about and The DARP team are proud to continue the work that he and I began.

I had become entirely disenchanted with a career as a commercial solicitor and David was looking towards a new venture in the wake of the Jackson Reforms. We had spoken in great detail about the newly evolving concept of Dispute Avoidance as early as 2013 and what that meant and how the ADR landscape might embrace such a notion when in reality the term 'Dispute Resolution' was relatively new itself. In early 2015 a solicitor and a Mediator combined their common beliefs and passions and The DARP was formed and moulded in our collective image of 'how can we help' those in dispute to manage and resolve their differences as efficiently and effectively as possible and ideally without recourse to the court system but also how can disputes be avoided in the first place.

We began writing articles and papers and delivering seminars and courses on how we believed that the avoidance, resolution and management of disputes should occur. These ultimately led us to the concept and development of this Guide.

When he and I began this journey we had no concept of how it would develop and grow or how much the ADR landscape would shift towards Dispute Avoidance and those conversations and discussions we had in 2013. With David Evans, Ian White, Stephen Hall, Wolf von Kumberg and Zaza Johnson Elsheikh joining as Consultants this has added further experiences and skillsets to The DARP team and we are all honoured and privileged to complete this Guide and dedicate it to David.

Oliver Richbell
Partner, The Dispute Avoidance & Resolution Partnership

The Dispute Avoidance & Resolution Partnership team have designed and written a series of courses and workshops on Dispute Avoidance, Dispute Management and Dispute Resolution which set the basis for this Guide. Each course and workshop can be tailored to meet any specific need and if you would wish to discuss how they can delivered to your business please contact us via office@thedarp.co.uk or on 01234 241 242.

Printed in Great Britain
by Amazon

39604361R00089